origami

origami

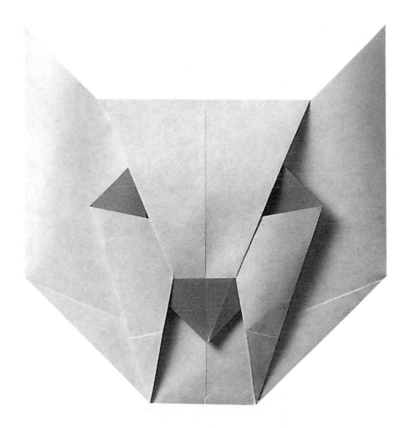

David Petty

Published by SILVERDALE BOOKS
An imprint of Bookmart Ltd
Registered number 2372865
Trading as Bookmart Ltd
Blaby Road
Wigston
Leicester LE18 4SE

© 2007 D&S Books Ltd

D&S Books Ltd
Kerswell,
Parkham Ash, Bideford
Devon, England
EX39 5PR

e-mail us at:- enquiries@d-sbooks.co.uk

ISBN 13: 9-781-84509-443-0

DS0150. Origami

Creative Director: Sarah King
Project Editor: Claire Bone
Designer: Debbie Fisher
Photographer: Colin Bowling/Paul Forrester

Fonts: Trebuchet MS and Myriad Tilt

Material from this book previously appeared in Origami 123 and Origami ABC

Printed in Thailand

1 3 5 7 9 10 8 6 4 2

contents

introduction

Origami in the West

In common with the origins of origami in the East, the origins of origami in the West are shrouded in the mists of time. Mere fragments of information are all that we have to build on. What can be said is the there was an early tradition of folding cloth in the form of clothing and napkins. In the 16th century, for instance, there are records of elaborate napkin-folding. Papyrus, the first form of paper in the West, was apparently foldable, as there is one example in Milan of an Egyptian folded map. Its preservation seems miraculous, but less important forms of paperwork have not survived.

During the 4th century, the popes were usually attended by ceremonial fans, or "flabelli", some of which were made from folded parchment.

Paper-folding had to wait until the secret of papermaking was passed on to Europe. Subsequent to this, some actual European paper folds were handed down, the most prominent being the pajarita (see page 171) and multi-form.

In around 1880 travellers from the East introduced the flapping bird (see page 177, 186) and the frog (see page 191). The German educator Friedrich Froebel (1782–1852) founded his kindergarten system in 1835, a part of which included European paper-folding, mainly based on geometric decorative folds. Froebel was building on the European tradition of paper-folding that was then prevalent.

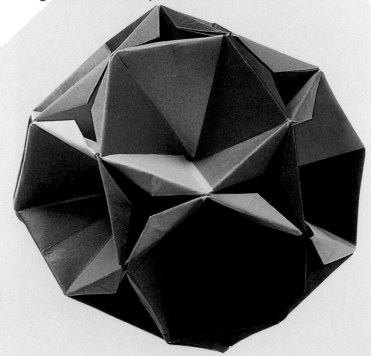

Paper-folding became a popular children's pastime in Victorian England, and John Tenniel's famous illustrations for *Through the Looking Glass*, by Lewis Carroll, feature two simple paper hats, one worn by the carpenter and the other, folded like a traditional boat, worn by the man dressed in white paper in the railway carriage. A depiction of a similarly folded hat can also be found in the detailed painting *A Little Nimrod*, by James Joseph Jacques Tissot (a French painter), of around 1882.

A major popularisation of origami was generated during the 1950s by Gershon Legman and Lilian Oppenheimer in the United States, and Robert Harbin in the UK. Between Harbin, Samuel Randlett (USA) and Akira Yoshizawa of Japan, an international categorisation of the symbols used in step diagrams to explain folding methods was developed. That system is still in use today. Harbin was a successful stage magician and travelled extensively, including to Japan, where he was exposed to the Eastern folding tradition.

Since then technical advances in the West have enormously increased the possibilities of models. Neil

Elias (USA) gave us box pleating, while Robert Lang (USA) and John Montroll (USA) have greatly extended the range of bases and the complexity of models. Though the style may not please everyone, the detailed models now produced are undoubtedly technically far superior to earlier works.

What can be demonstrated is that origami still holds a special attraction. It is not only children who marvel at the transformation of an ordinary flat sheet of paper into something unexpected.

Accuracy

The more accurately you fold, the better the shape of the final model, but please don't get hung up on absolute accuracy. The best approach is to fold freely, then, when the steps are familiar, to try to improve the accuracy. The second attempt is invariably better than the first and the third is most likely better still. The whole point is to enjoy the experience.

Paper

Any paper can be used for origami (the cheaper the better when practising a new model!) Some models depend on a contrast between the two sides of the paper. It is best to use commercial paper for such models. Some models work best with foil-backed paper for stiffness. Choosing a suitable paper is part of the experience of origami. I recommend a plain paper to begin with, as location points can merge into the background on patterned paper.

Models

The models chosen utilise a wide variety of techniques. This is intended to give the reader a thorough grounding in the available techniques. If you persevere, then you should be ready to tackle any published model.

Final words –

enjoy yourself,

and happy folding

◆ origami creativity

Introduction

One of the unstated aims of this book is to encourage creators. This page is aimed solely at creation of origami models. Creation of new models cannot be taught. Latent creative skills can be developed. Understanding how the creative process works can help.

The four main creative strands

I have recognised several common threads both from my own experience and when talking to other creators. The following are in no particular order.

1. The improvement ploy

Most creations come from adapting existing examples. In origami terms, produce a variation of an existing model which has different properties. This stems from the idea that the existing can and should be improved. Several times I've seen new models without cuts developed from previous models which had cuts.

2. The creative play ploy

In origami terms, start with a paper, make a couple of moves then see if the shape of the paper suggests part or whole of a model. Make more moves until something is suggested. Work towards enhancing the shape to achieve the final model. With practice recognition of embryonic models becomes second nature.

3. The goal setting ploy

Deciding on a final target then working towards it can be very effective. In origami terms, the final model is decided first, then the most suitable starting point (or points) chosen with the target in mind. What follows must inevitably be the perspiration from the phrase "Creation is 10% inspiration and 90% perspiration." A variation of this ploy is to decide both the overall goal and the starting point i.e. I want to make a modular piece using a particular base (fish, bird, kite waterbomb etc.).

4. Serendipity

I define this as the rare occasions when a complete solution springs into mind, almost out of the blue. This process usually gives the best results. Invariably the moment of realisation must have been preceded by a period of preparation. In origami terms, working with a few selected techniques gives familiarity and can trigger a spontaneous creative surge. Models suggested this way need only a little extra work to complete.

Creativity in practice

Which path to follow?

There is no single way to create. Creation is an imprecise art. Usually several of the processes outlined above are employed together in the creation of a single model. The path to follow is the one (or ones) which suit you best. The important thing is to keep trying, it does get easier with practice.

Other creative aides

Inspiration can be triggered in many ways. Adopting a favourite technique, perhaps, and developing a new model using that technique. Taking a new tack, i.e. tackling a subject nobody has yet done, or tackling an old subject from a fresh viewpoint. Brainstorming as a technique can open up new viewpoint ideas. Be open to sources outside origami and be prepared to adapt them. Set a new target — fold a recognisable model in only five steps, for example. Perhaps you might consider a change of philosophy — start with a triangular paper, or allow more than one piece in the finished model. Dare to do something different.

When creating a complex model, try splitting the model into smaller parts and work on each part separately. The separate papers can be fixed together later and any anomalies worked out.

Don't let yourself be sidetracked. Ignore all the exciting distractions of which paper to choose, what colour to fold with, etc. Do it the hard way: use brown wrapping paper (if it's an animal, say) or your most infrequently used coloured paper (if you need colour contrast). This way, you are more likely to make models that are independent of the paper used. If you need a few incentives, then consider these. Creators get their work published in society publications (free books/magazines, free convention packs). Better creators get their work published for real (money, prestige, etc.) Go for it.

The creative cycle

The first step is learning basic techniques. In origami terms, this means folding everything and anything you can get hold of. The next step is usually improving existing models. The inspiration for this is in the form of "What if this model had a better property (shape, movement, etc.)?" The final step is producing your own complete models.

There is another "maturity" cycle which usually applies too, once some creative proficiency is achieved. Most creators discover that once they can improve on existing models then complex models are relatively easy to create. After a period of complex creations, realisation dawns that, paradoxically, good simple models are even more difficult to create. Good simple models are rare. This is no coincidence.

Most creators go through creative highs and lows. During a high period models are tumble out at a faster rate than can be folded or diagrammed. Inevitably,

after a high there follows a low or fallow period when inspiration is lacking. The experience is (I imagine) similar to writer's block.

Goodness and badness

I define the term "good" as applied to an origami model as:

- instantly recognisable final model (strong outline)
- pleasing folding sequence
- economic use of paper
- easily obtainable starting paper size
- final model pleasing to the eye
- no design weaknesses (e.g. split back on animal).

The term "bad" as applied to an origami model is the opposite to "good", that is:

- poorly recognisable final model (weak outline)
- unpleasant folding sequence
- uneconomic use of paper
- awkward starting paper size
- ugly to look at
- design weaknesses are apparent.

There are good models in all classes, simple, intermediate and complex. One thought strikes me. More people are likely to fold a good simple model than a good intermediate or good complex model. Popularity is only one criteria of the success of a model. Critical acclaim is another. As in all artistic activities, there are no hard and fast rules; there are general guidelines perhaps or rules that only exist for breaking. Do your own thing.

Happy folding and creating!
David Petty

◆folds and bases ....

Before beginning the models, you should familiarise yourself with some of the basic folds. The main ones you will encounter are:

Valley fold

This is the basis for all origami models. For this you bring one edge of the paper up to meet the other — thus creating a "valley".

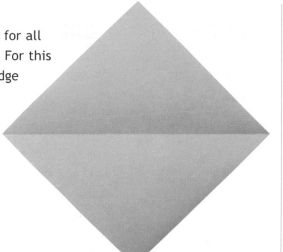

Mountain fold

This is the reverse of the valley fold. Here you fold one edge of the paper underneath the other — creating a "mountain".

There are also a number of bases and folds which form steps for many models. Steps for creating these are as follows:

Kite base

This is the easiest base, named after the shape it forms. Simply fold both edges of the sheet to meet the centre line. Make sure both edges are lined up evenly before creasing firmly.

Squash

You will need to practise this, as it is very easy to wrinkle.

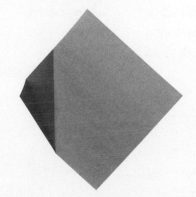

1 Take a 2x1 sheet folded in half to make a square of double thickness.

2 Take the edge of the paper to the crease, valley fold and return.

3 Separate the layers and gently squash down on the top of the flap, flattening it evenly.

Petal fold

Begin with the squash fold.

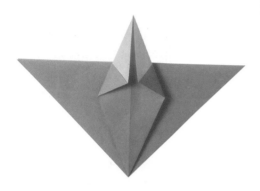

1 Fold both corners of the squash to the centre and return.

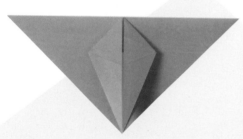

2 Mountain fold these corners inside. Lift the bottom point of the flap to meet the top. Make sure your creases are even, and firmly made.

Rabbit-ear fold

Commonly used to create ears, this fold makes a small moveable flap.

1 Fold the corners of the square to the centre and return.

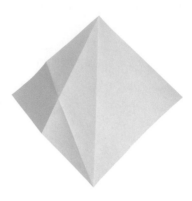

2 Fold the second corners of the square to the centre and return.

3 Fold both corners of the square to the centre.

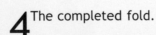

4 The completed fold.

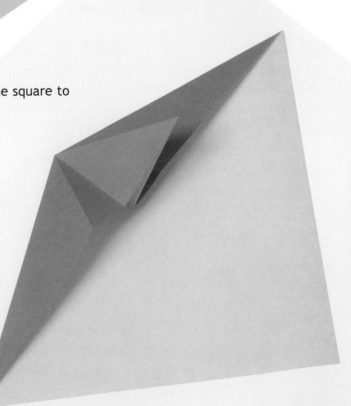

Inside reverse fold

Reverse folds are where you reverse the direction of a previous crease.

1 Starting with a square with diagonal centre fold, fold the tip at an angle. The point should lay outside the vertical edge.

2 Return the tip.

3 Open the layers and gently press the tip down. It is easy to crinkle this fold, so take care to only use the original creases.

4 To complete, bring the layers together again.

Outside reverse fold

Here the fold is outside the main part of the paper.

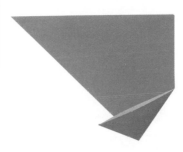

1 Begin with a square with a central diagonal fold. Fold the tip at an angle, with point laying outside the vertical edge.

2 Return the tip.

3 Open the layers and gently push the tip backwards. Use only existing creases.

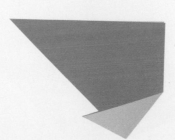

4 To complete, bring layers together again.

Inside crimp

Begin with a kite base, mountain-folded in half.

1 Choose an angle, then valley fold tip.

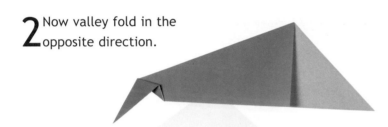

2 Now valley fold in the opposite direction.

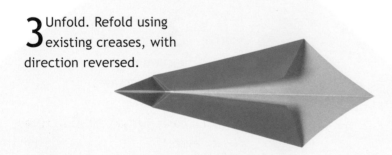

3 Unfold. Refold using existing creases, with direction reversed.

4 Side view.

Outside crimp.

Begin in same way as inside crimp.

1 Valley fold tip to an angle.

2 Valley fold in the opposite direction. Unfold.

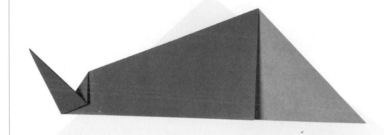

3 Now refold using existing creases, in the opposite direction.

Waterbomb base

Start with a square, valley-folded from left to right.

1 Mountain fold top edge to bottom. Then valley fold diagonally top left corner to bottom right corner. Then diagonally valley fold top right to bottom left corner.

2 Push all creases into the centre and gently flatten the paper as shown.

Squash fold

Here the fold is outside the main part of the paper.

1 Fold left edge to centre and return.

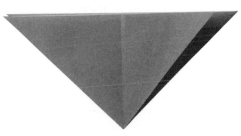

2 Lift the flap upright, separate the layers and push down to flatten.

Blintz base

Start with square with two diagonal creases.

1 Valley fold each corner to the centre point.

2 Fold creases firmly, ensuring edges stay even.

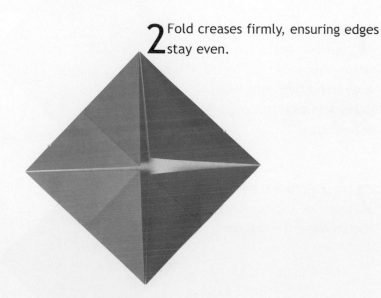

Fish base

Begin with a square, crease diagonally in half twice.

1 Create kite base.

2 Fold top tip down to meet the bottom tip. Mountain and valley fold as shown.

3 Lift the front flap along the crease.

4 Turn over for completed base.

Preliminary base

Begin with a square sheet, creased diagonally.

1 Mountain fold top corner to bottom and return. Valley fold top left edge to bottom right edge. Valley fold top right edge to bottom left edge.

2 Bring all four corners together and carefully flatten along the crease.

Windmill base

Named for the shape it creates. Begin with a square sheet, creased in half both ways.

1 Valley fold top edge to centre line. Repeat with bottom edge.

2 Fold both ends to centre line.

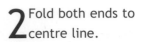

3 Pull out each corner in turn.

4 Thus creating four flaps.

5 To complete, valley fold two of the flaps.

Bird base (1)

This is a tricky base that begins with the preliminary base.

1 Valley fold left and right corners to centre and return. Mountain fold top corner to the back and return.

2 Raise the bottom flap of the front layer and bring it to the top.

3 This is the result.

4 Turn over and fold the middle flap up.

5 Again lift the bottom flap of the front layer only and bring it to the top.

6 Fold down the top tips of both the top and bottom layers.

7 The completed base.

Stretched bird base

A variation on the previous bird base.

1 Begin with the standard bird base.

2 Turn over and rotate the base. Gently pull the inner flaps until the bottom point pops inside.

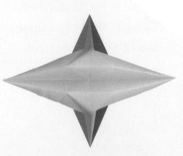

3 Flatten to complete.

Bird base (2)

Fold a square in half both ways. Note that for this base the coloured
side of the paper is face up.

1 Fold all four corners to the centre.

2 Form a preliminary base, with flaps face up.

3 On the top layer only, fold the sides to the centre and return. Make sure that the closed end is at the top.

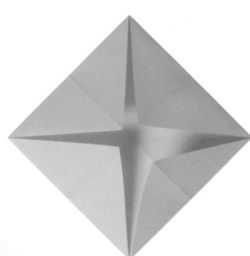

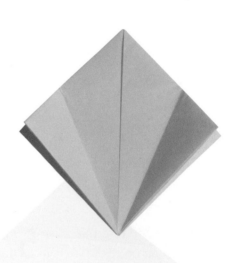

4 Petal fold front and back. Raise the upper layer and the sides will follow.

5 Pull out the hidden corners.

6 Fold the flaps down at both front and back.

7 Completed base.

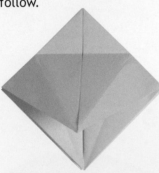

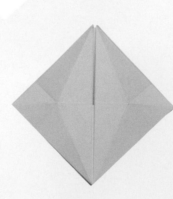

Sink fold

There are many valley and mountain folds in this, so make sure you are doing the right fold at the right time! Begin with a square, folded in half.

1 Form the waterbomb base with the colour on the outside.

2 Fold front tip to the middle of the bottom edge, firmly crease and return. Turn over and repeat. This clearly marks your creases.

3 Open out your sheet and check the creases.

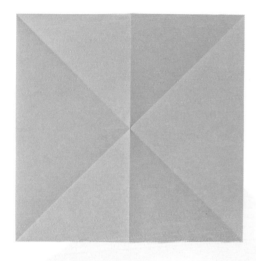

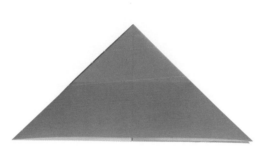

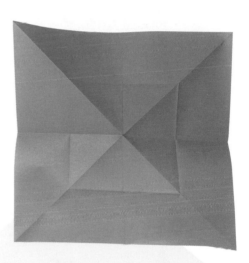

4 Now you need to put in a series of mountain folds, working round the sheet. First put in mountain folds in the outer corners, and then in the central square.

5 Push the sides towards the middle, at the same time as pushing down in the centre.

6 Taking care to line up the folds exactly, continue bringing the corners together.

7 Completed.

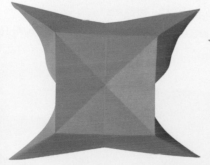

Double sink fold

A variation on the previous fold — with double the number of folds used!

1 Form waterbomb base as before, with colour on the outside.

2 Fold top tip to middle of bottom edge, crease and return. Repeat on the other side.

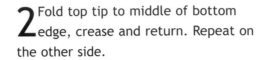

3 Fold the tip to this new crease, crease firmly and return. Repeat on other side.

4 Open out the sheet and again work round putting in mountain folds in the outer corners and inner square.

5 Push in from the sides, at the same time as pushing down in the centre to bring the corners together.

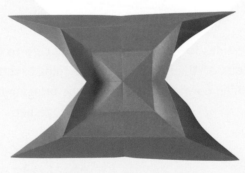

6 Partially open out to the single sink.

7 Push the centre up to form the shape as shown.

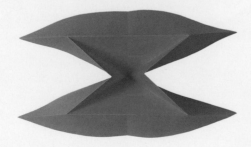

8 Bring corners together — ensure you maintain the creases.

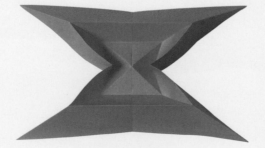

9 Completed.

Frog base

This is probably the most complicated of the bases and you will need a lot of practice!

1 Form the preliminary base.

2 Squash the right tip of the top layer.

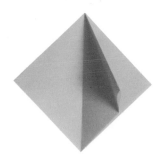

3 Using existing creases, swing this flap to the other side.

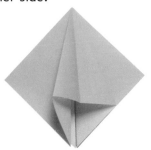

4 Squash the left tip of the top layer in the same way.

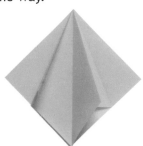

5 Check all your creases are even and made firmly.

6 Turn over and squash right tip as before.

7 Swing this flap to the other side.

8 Squash left tip as before.

9 Valley fold the edges to the centre and return. Make sure the creases go exactly to the point. Raise the top layer along a line that joins the folded edges, and petal fold.

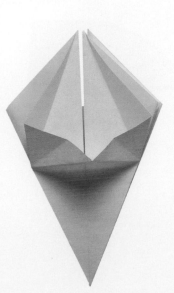

10 Petal fold shown half way.

11 Repeat the petal fold on three more flaps to complete.

Portrait base ERIC KENNEWAY

This is another complicated base, which will require plenty of practice!

1 Precrease.

2 Precrease vertical, fold horizontal.

3 Inside reverse fold.

4 Precrease.

5 Squash.

6 Fold tip to point.

7 Fold edge to crease.

8 Swivel fold, pulling material from under triangle.

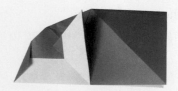

9 Fold flap back.

10 Rotate squash portion, turn over.

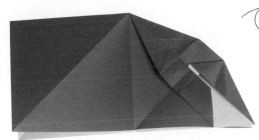

11 Repeat steps 7–9 on left hand side.

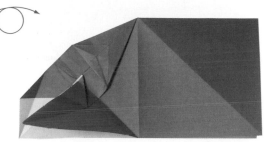

12 Rotate squash portion.

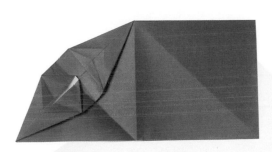

13 Squash.

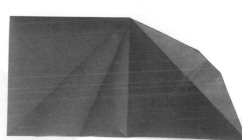

14 Squash flap hidden inside to form nose.

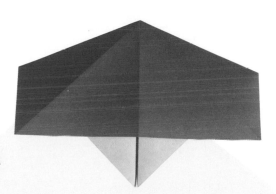

Portrait base inverted

It is necessary to open the model to swing the front flap over and behind.

1 basic models

The first projects are some of the simplest to create and will allow you to gain confidence in your folding before moving on to some of the more complex models.

Dart

This is one of the easiest models to make, and is one which many people make without even realising they're creating an origami model! No special paper is required, as a sheet of A4 paper is perfectly suitable.

 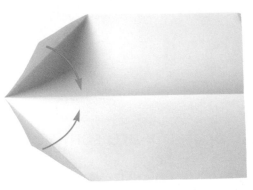 

1 Bring the long edges together, crease and unfold.

2 Bring the short edges to the centre crease, using diagonal valley folds.

3 Bring the folded edges to the centre crease, again using valley folds. Ensure that the already folded corners do not creep.

4 Fold the model in half, hiding the folds.

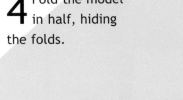

5 Fold down the wings at right angles. Ensure that you make the folds in the same place on each side.

Banger

A traditional model much loved by schoolchildren! Again, a sheet of A4 paper is ideal, as the paper needs to be thin, but strong.

1 Crease both the horizontal and vertical centre lines and return.

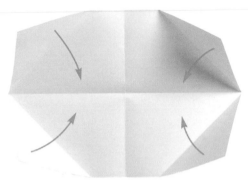

2 Fold the corners down to the longer centre line.

3 Fold the model in half with a valley fold. The corners are inside.

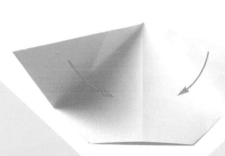

4 Now fold the top corners to the centre line.

5 Fold the model in half again, this time with a mountain fold.

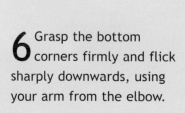

6 Grasp the bottom corners firmly and flick sharply downwards, using your arm from the elbow.

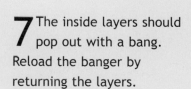

7 The inside layers should pop out with a bang. Reload the banger by returning the layers.

Boat/snapper

Two models in one! Another design that can be easily folded using a sheet of A4. Here we start with a rectangle with a central vertical fold.

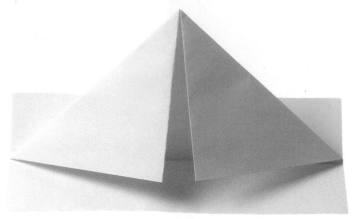

1 Fold the sheet horizontally.

2 Now fold the two top corners down to the centre line.

3 Fold the bottom edge of the top layer up to the top as far as possible. Make sure that you keep this even. Repeat with the back layer.

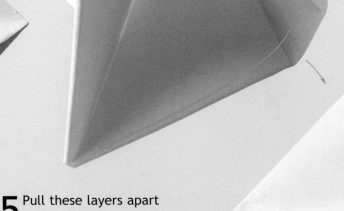

4 Pull the layers apart and flatten the model. Fold the bottom point of the top layer up to meet the top point. Repeat with the back layer.

5 Pull these layers apart and flatten.

6 Fold the bottom point of the top layer to meet the top point. Repeat with the back layer.

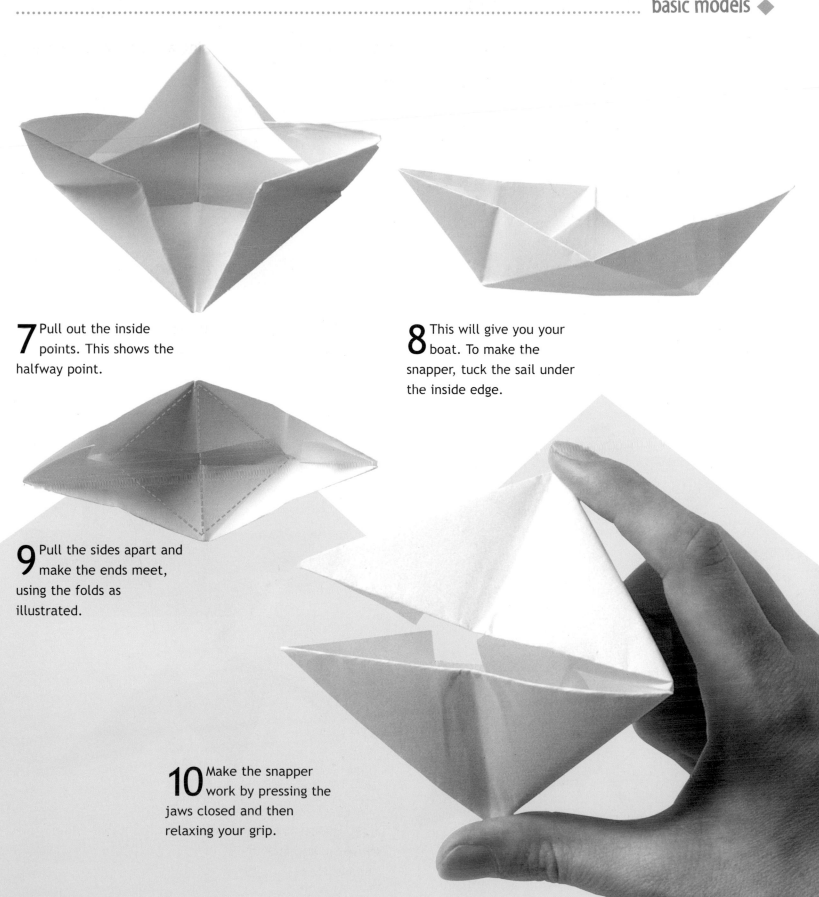

7 Pull out the inside points. This shows the halfway point.

8 This will give you your boat. To make the snapper, tuck the sail under the inside edge.

9 Pull the sides apart and make the ends meet, using the folds as illustrated.

10 Make the snapper work by pressing the jaws closed and then relaxing your grip.

Fluttering butterfly

Watch as this beautiful model takes flight and transforms before your eyes into a delicate butterfly.

1 Crease both diagonals. Leave one folded.

2 Fold folded edge over (approximately 1/3).

4 Fold wings down at right angles from point at which front edge of wing meets diagonal.

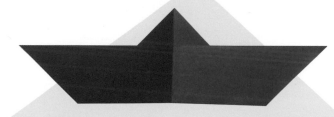

3 Valley fold in half.

5 Launch as an aeroplane model and it will rotate to the ground.

Folder

Here's an invaluable way of storing secret treasures or mementos of an occasion past, but never forgotten.

1 Crease centreline. Fold corner to hit centreline. Cut off above the meeting point *A4-size sheet*:start at step 2. *Square sheet*: start step 1.

2 Fold sides to centre and return. Fold corners to new creases. Fold sides to centre again.

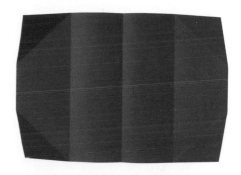

3 Fold top part behind turn over.

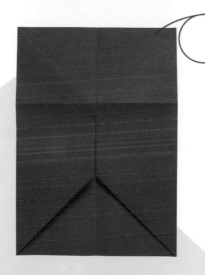

4 Fold bottom part up (crease lies at top of 45 degree edges behind) and tuck into top pockets.

5 Valley fold in half.

6 2 pockets 2 pockets 1 big or 4 small pockets inside

Mitre

A simple design to create a miter; this is great fun for children when made out of newspaper and playing dress up.

1 Crease lengthways. Fold short edges together.

2 Fold double thickness.

3 Result. Turn over.

4 Fold to centreline.

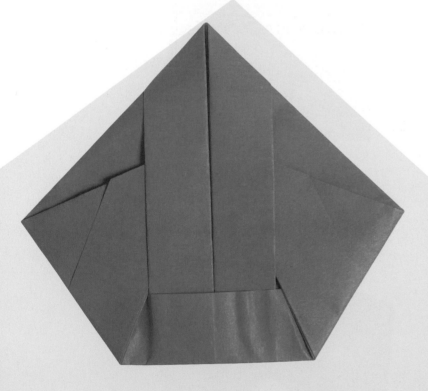

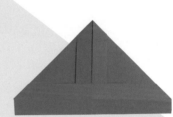

5 Fold top layer up.

6 Fold points behind, fold bottom layer behind.

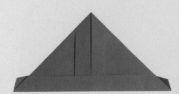

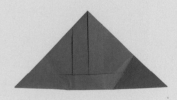

7 Fold points between layers.

8 Fold points under central strips.

House

difficulty :

origin :
traditional

This design can be made using any size origami paper. The house can be decorated by drawing in windows and doors if you wish. It begins with a square with a vertical crease. As with most models, the white side of the paper is face up.

1 Fold the origami paper in half horizontally.

2 Fold the short edges to the centre.

3 Open the top layer and squash the top corners.

Organ

difficulty :

origin :
traditional

A fun model that begins with the completed house model. This can also be decorated by drawing in keys if you wish.

1 Fold up the central section of the house so that the edge meets the top edge.

2 Crease this folded section, lifting up white area, and return.

3 Fold the top edge of this section down to meet the crease you created in step 2.

4 Now fold along the crease made in step 2.

5 Fold the sides at right angles. Now fold the "keyboard" down at right angles too.

House envelope

An original design that follows on from the house model. It involves lots of quite small folds, so to begin with at least you may wish to practise this on larger origami paper. It begins with a square, creased vertically in half.

2 Fold the sides to the centre and squash the top corners.

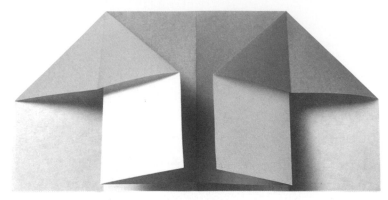

1 Fold the square horizontally in half.

3 Fold the flaps you've created to the outside, trapping the coloured triangles between the layers.

4 Now fold the bottom edges up to the centre.

5 Fold the top edges down. Ensure that the corners are free.

6 Fold the flaps in towards the middle, using existing creases.

7 Fold the bottom flap up and tuck it in.

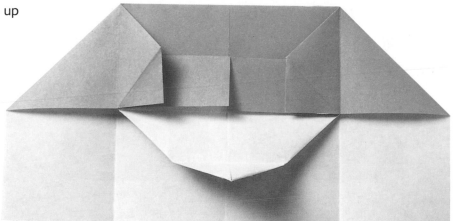

8 Now fold the sides into the centre.

9 Fold the bottom corners into the centre.

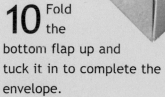

10 Fold the bottom flap up and tuck it in to complete the envelope.

Happicoat

This traditional model turns itself into a beautiful yet simple Japanese kimono.

Using two-sided paper gives it a particularly pleasing effect.

1 Crease centrelines. Fold top edge to lower edge.

2 Fold and return.

3 Fold to crease.

4 Fold top layer only.

5 Result. Turn over and rotate.

6 Fold down.

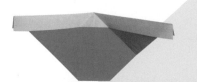

7 Fold to centreline.

8 Result, turn over.

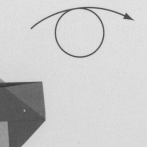

9 Raise lower layer and pull side flaps out.

10 Result. Turn over.

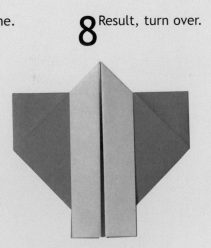

11 Complete.

Snapper

This design uses a waterbomb base; great fun for children to make and play with and discover origami for themselves.

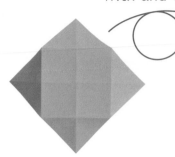  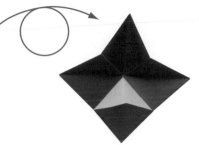 

1 Fold corners to centre. Turn over.

2 Fold corners to centre. Turn over.

3 Form waterbomb base, lifting top flap.

4 To make snap, hold either side of head, push hands together, then return.

Star box

A 3D design in a star shape to collect little treasures and keepsakes.

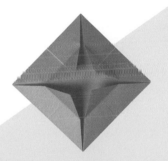  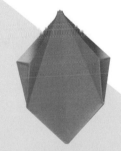

1 Form preliminary base.

2 Fold sides to centre, squash lower part, repeat at back.

3 Bookfold front and back.

4 Fold sides to centre, repeat at back.

5 Fold and return lower triangle.

6 Fold point down. Repeat on all four sides.

7 Insert finger to form box.

2 containers

The projects in this chapter include a variety of different boxes, from the very simple to the more complicated, as well as some more unusual containers.

difficulty :

origin :
traditional

Simple box

This box is called *masu* in Japanese, which means "measuring box". It may require some practice to make the sides even, but you will have a pretty display box.

1 Crease the square in half both vertically and horizontally and return.

2 Fold each corner to the centre — you have created the blintz base.

3 Fold all sides to the centre and return.

4 Now open the two opposite corners of the blintz base.

5 Lift the sides so that they are vertical.

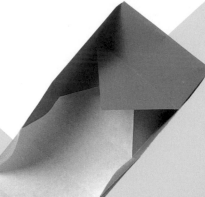

6 Now lift one of the remaining ends. This brings the model into three dimensions. Fold the flap at the raised end into the centre. It traps the coloured triangles.

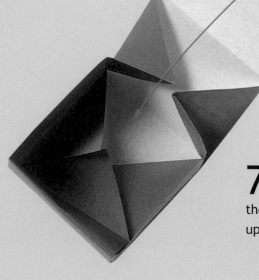

7 Raise the remaining end and fold the flap of this end into the centre. You may have to firm up your creases to finish off.

Multi-box

.... containers ◆

Another traditional display box, which gets its name from the multiplicity of rectangles that it can be folded from.

 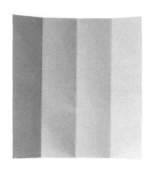  

1 Crease the vertical centre line.

2 Fold the left- and right-hand edges to the centre line.

3 Fold back a strip of each flap.

4 Now fold both strips back again.

5 Fold each of the four corners to the crease that is formed by folding the strips.

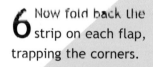

6 Now fold back the strip on each flap, trapping the corners.

7 Lift the layers on each side to open the box. You may need to firm up the creases to make a sharp box shape.

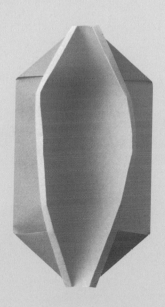

House box

This project uses the ever-versatile house model as its basis. It begins with a square sheet, creased horizontally in half. The coloured side of the paper should be face up.

1 Mountain-fold the square in half, retaining the colour on the outside.

2 Fold the sides to the centre and squash the top corners.

3 Fold the flaps to the outside, trapping the triangles in the layers.

4 Fold the bottom edges to the centre. Repeat on both sides.

5 Fold the top edges down, ensuring that the corners are free.

6 Fold up the front flap and tuck it inside. Repeat at the back.

7 Press on the ridge at the top and pull into three dimensions. Now turn over.

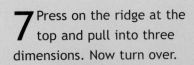

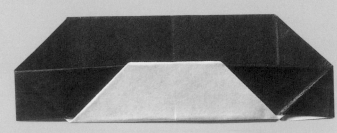

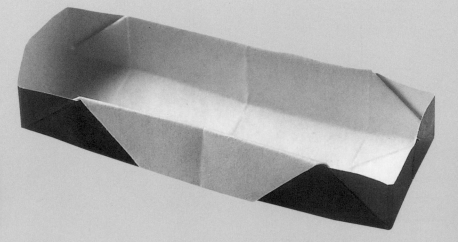

Drinking cup .... containers ◆

This model can be made in any size, and, like the drinking cup after which it is named, will actually hold water, although probably not for very long!

 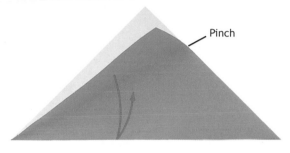 Pinch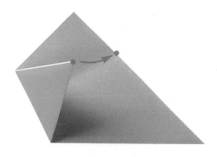

1 First fold the square diagonally, using a valley fold.

2 Take the top flap down to the bottom edge, but pinch only at the edge and do not crease.

3 Take the left-hand corner to the pinch on the right-hand edge so that the marked points meet.

4 Now take the right-hand corner to the left-hand end so that the marked points meet.

5 Fold the upper corner of the top layer down to the front.

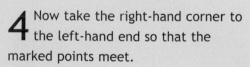
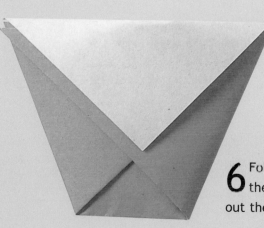

6 Fold the remaining upper flap to the rear. Use your finger to open out the cup.

Waterbomb

The waterbomb is a classic traditional design and one that will be familiar to many people. It is probably better to practise making it using larger paper to give yourself room to make all of the folds neatly.

 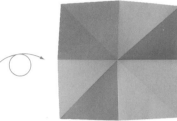 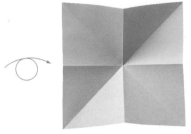 

1 Fold both diagonals and return. Turn over.

2 Fold the horizontal and vertical centre lines and then return.

3 Turn the paper over and then collapse it along the creases.

4 Fold the tips of the top layer to the top. Repeat at the rear.

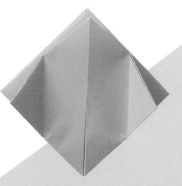  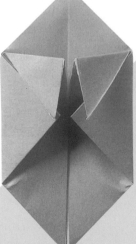

7 Now fold and tuck these flaps into the little pockets that you've created. Gently press on the edge to open the pockets. Repeat at the rear.

5 Fold the left- and right-hand corners to the centre. Repeat at the rear.

6 Fold the top tips down. Now repeat at the rear.

 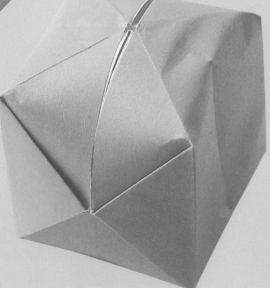

8 Separate the layers and blow into the hole at the bottom. You may find it helpful to fold and return the top and bottom points at the centre to ease the final shaping.

Complex box .... containers ◆

We have already seen a simple box construction. However, once you have mastered the simple box, you may enjoy the number of complex folds in this variation. It begins with the paper's coloured side face up.

1 Crease the diagonals and blintz in and return all four corners.

2 Crease and return the corners to meet the blintz creases.

3 Turn the paper over. Fold and return the left- and right-hand corners to meet your original blintz creases. Fold in the top and bottom corners to meet the blintzed creases. Then fold the top and bottom edges along the blintz creases so that the edge lies along the crease that forms the central square.

4 Crease the top left-hand edge along the imaginary line formed between the bottom left-hand corner of the top coloured band and the bottom of the left-hand crease you created in step 3. Repeat on the other three edges.

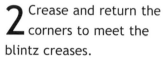 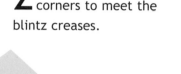

5 Turn the paper over. Fold the sides at right angles and waterbomb the ends (see page 15 for instructions).

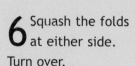

6 Squash the folds at either side. Turn over.

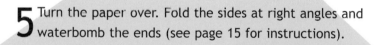

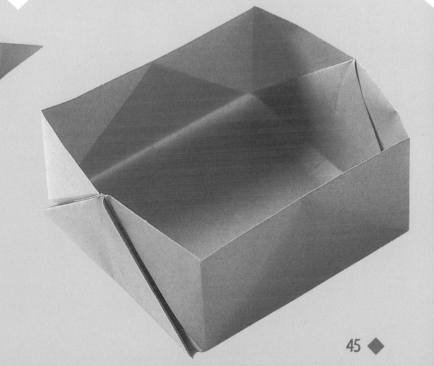

Sanbow

To the Japanese, the sanbow is an offering tray. It is a complex model to make, but the result is a delicate and decorative box.

1 First crease and return both diagonal centre lines. Then create a blintz base, coloured side out (see page 15), turn over and mountain-fold in half.

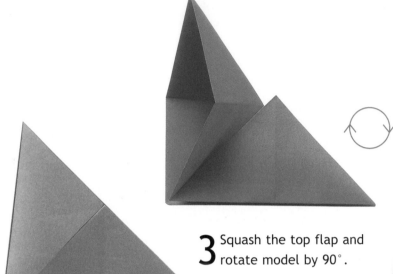

2 Now valley-fold the flap up to a right angle.

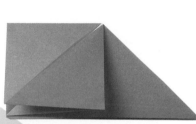

3 Squash the top flap and rotate model by 90°.

4 This will give you a right-hand flap.

5 Turn the model over and again fold the flap up to a right angle.

6 Now squash the top flap.

7 Lift the front corner up, opening out the side flaps as you do so.

8 Once you have flattened out the flaps, turn the model over.

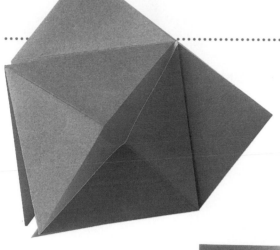

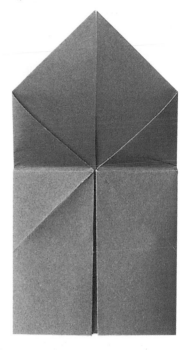

9 Lift the front flap and open out the side flaps as in step 7.

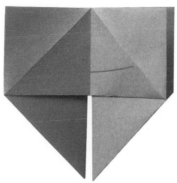

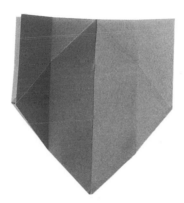

10 Fold the top right layer over to the left. Now turn over and do the same at the rear. This is a book fold.

11 Now fold both sides in to the centre line, front and rear.

12 Rotate the model so that the point is at the top. Fold down the top front flap so that the point meets the bottom edge. Repeat at the rear.

13 Pull the front and rear flaps out to open out the sanbow.

Lazy Susan

A lazy Susan is a food-serving container. It was so called because the dish provided a way of storing several items ready for visitors, thus saving time. This is an unusual model in that it has curved sides.

1 With the coloured side of the paper face up, crease the centre lines horizontally and vertically.

2 Now crease both diagonal centre lines.

3 Now fold in all four corners to the centre to create a blintz.

4 Fold the four corners to the outside edges.

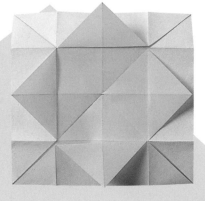

5 Mountain-fold along the sides of the central square and then fold out into three dimensions.

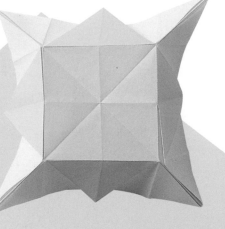

6 Push the centre downwards, and at the same time push the sides inwards.

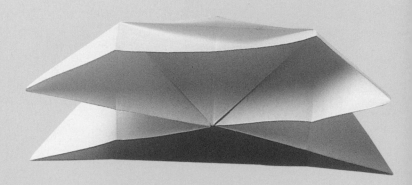

7 This is the shape that you should finish up with.

8 Inside reverse-fold both of the front tips.

9 Now inside reverse-fold both of the back tips.

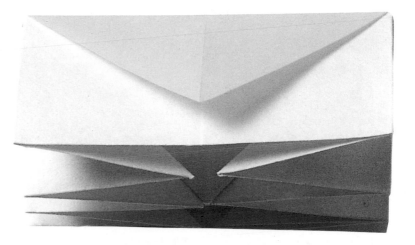

10 This is how your model should look at this stage.

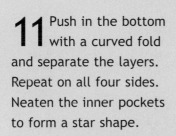

11 Push in the bottom with a curved fold and separate the layers. Repeat on all four sides. Neaten the inner pockets to form a star shape.

difficulty :

origin :

david petty

Rota cup

A very detailed model, intended for practised folders. A great food container in which to carry anything from sweets to biscuits — even delicious fish and chips!

1 Crease centrelines.

2 Mountain fold on third lines.

3 Add valley folds to third lines.

4 Mountain fold central square and raise centre.

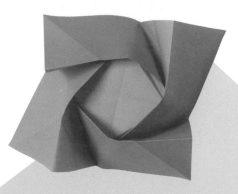

5 Tuck flaps between layers.

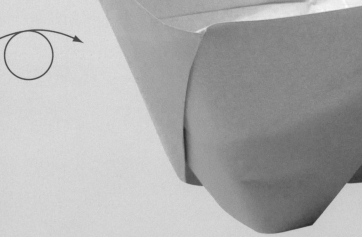

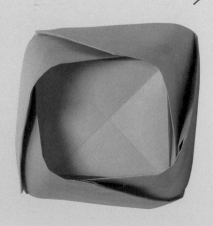

6 Turn over.

7 Complete. This is an example of twist folding.

Pencil holder

Do you always have pencils and pens lying around the house and never the right container to store them in? Well here is the model to solve your problem. With some complex folds — expanded to 3D at the end — we recommend you use thin strong paper and it will last and last.

1 Form preliminary base.

2 Fold edges to centreline. Repeat at rear.

3 Fold and return edges to centreline. Repeat at rear.

4 Unfold side flaps, valley fold and return lower point.

  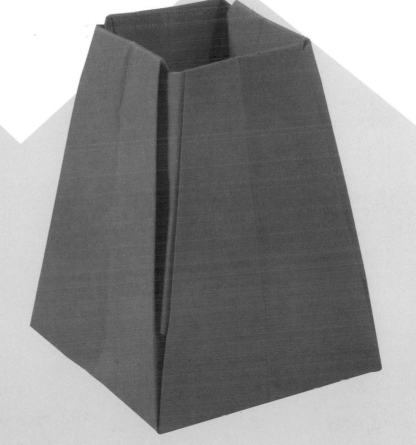

5 Double inside reverse all four flaps.

6 Fold flaps inside, point coincides with reverses.

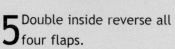 

7 Tuck each flap into a pocket.

8 Put finger inside and expand to 3D. Lower tip will rise and flatten.

Basket with handles

A wonderful way of holding gifts for Mother's Day or birthdays is this traditional model of a basket with handles.

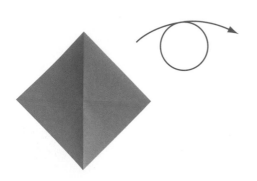

1 Crease diagonals. Turn over.

2 Crease centrelines. Turn over.

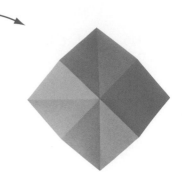

3 Form preliminary base.

4 Fold flaps down, front and back.

5 Fold tip to edge, front and back.

6 Result. Add handle.

Note: handle touches white top flaps and tucks inside lower coloured triangular flaps.

handle

1 Fold sides to centre.

2 Repeat.

3 Fold in half.

4 Fold in half.

5 Fold edge to centre, folding handle too, front and back.

6 Fold corners inside to centre.

7 Fold flaps down.

8 3D basket part.

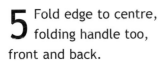

9 Round handle at top, fold side flaps inside.

Top view.

Container

This model starts off with a waterbomb base. It is a complex model to make, but the result is a strong and versatile container.

Start — preliminary base

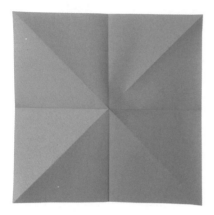

1 Precrease waterbomb base.

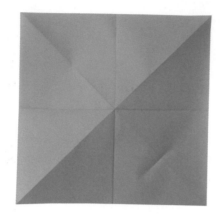

2 Mark quarter diagonals.

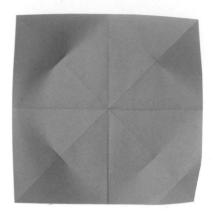

3 Mark eighth diagonals.

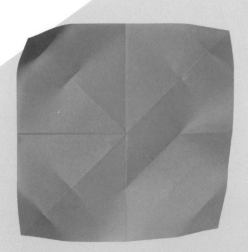

4 Fold each quadrant.

5 Fold each quadrant then turn over.

6 Pinch centres of two adjacent sides, raising central square, then work around other sides.

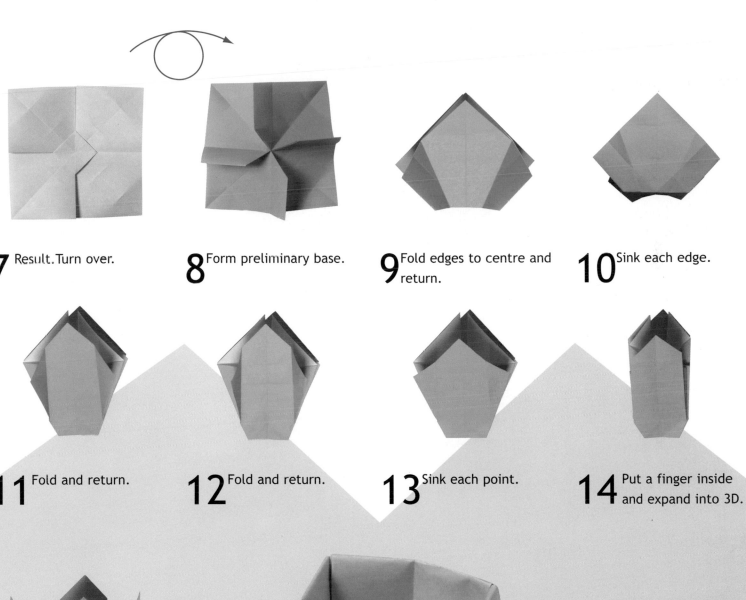

7 Result. Turn over.

8 Form preliminary base.

9 Fold edges to centre and return.

10 Sink each edge.

11 Fold and return.

12 Fold and return.

13 Sink each point.

14 Put a finger inside and expand into 3D.

15 Tuck tips between side and inside square.

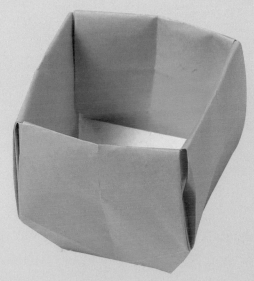

Fancy box

A traditional model, which is beautiful to look at and to make; the perfect way to complement any gift for a friend or loved one.

1 Precrease diagonals then blintz.

2 Result. Turn over.

3 Blintz again.

4 Fold corners to outer edge.

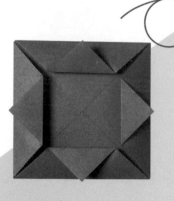

5 Result. Turn over.

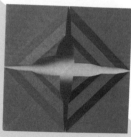

6 Pleat (sixths).

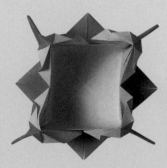

7 Press sides together at corners to form box.

8 Complete.

Seed packet

.... containers ◆

This is a really simple but versatile model. Useful when splitting seeds for planting or for storage. Fold with any rectangle.

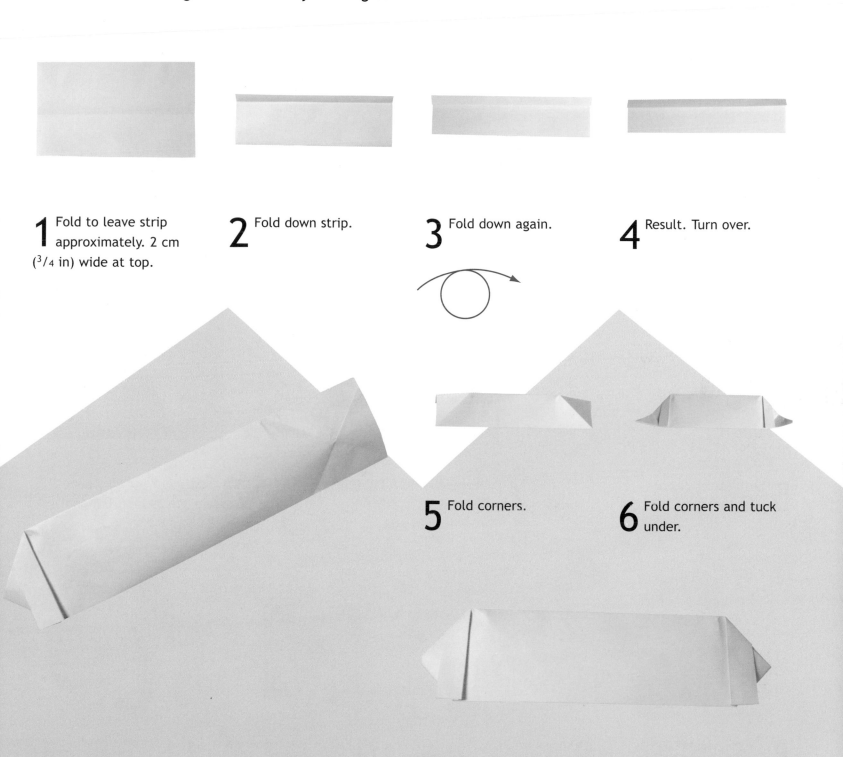

1 Fold to leave strip approximately. 2 cm (³/₄ in) wide at top.

2 Fold down strip.

3 Fold down again.

4 Result. Turn over.

5 Fold corners.

6 Fold corners and tuck under.

7 Result. Open end to put in seeds, then close again.

Fancy basket

A traditional yet simple design, it will delight anyone who will be amazed at its complexity. But don't tell anyone — it's your secret!

1 Crease both diagonals.

2 Crease horizontal and vertical.

3 Fold edges to centre and return.

4 Fold corners to centre at back and return.

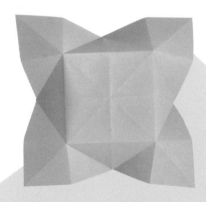

5 Fold centres of edges to centre.

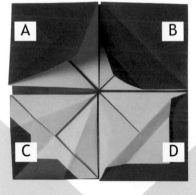

6 Follow sequence A-B-C-D on all corners.

7 Result. Fold a second paper, same size as first, but omit step 6d.

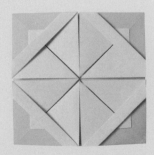

8 Cut the second sheet.

9 Shows result.

10 Follow the sequence a-b as shown for each part of the second sheet.

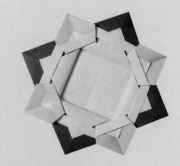

11 Final composite. Turn over.

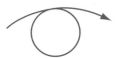

handle

12 Push in the sides.

13 To 3D the model, turn over — mountain folds at corners are hard folds — these can be soft folds.

1 Roll a same size paper to form a handle.

2 Squash roll flat, then tuck strip between layers.

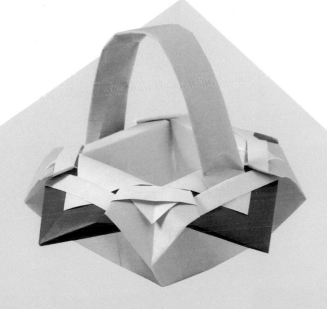

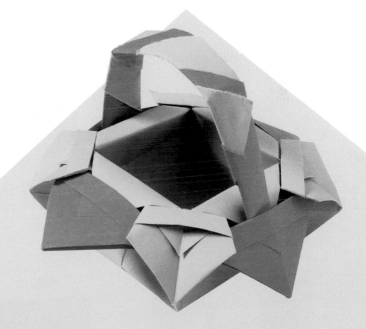

Chinese vase

This is an advanced model and requires complex folding; watch it unfold before your eyes into a beautiful vase.

1 Crease into thirds.

2 Add halfway creases.

3 Add more halfway creases.

4 Pleat.

5 Pleat.

6 Result; turn over.

7 Result.

8a Enlarged view. Collapse on existing creases.

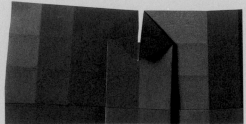

8b Lift and squash the end of each pleat.

9 Result. Turn over.

10 Crease and return.

11 Fold sides to centre.

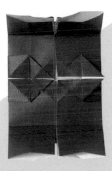

12 Fold edges to centre, tuck into pockets.

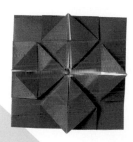

13 Fold corners inside.

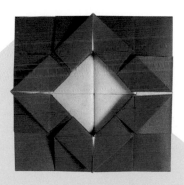

14 Result. Turn over.

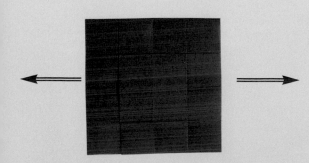

15 Tease out the paper trapped in the pleats. Work round evenly, a little at a time.

3 novelty models

These models are particularly fun to make, and with a little experimentation with folds and use of colour you can create your own variations.

Japanese helmet

A simple, yet effective, design that creates the traditional Japanese warrior's helmet.

It can be combined with the page-marker base on pages 76—77 for a different effect.

1 Fold the paper in half along the diagonal.

2 Fold down both top corners to meet the bottom corner.

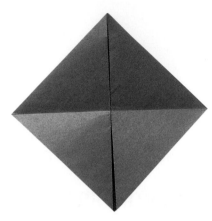

3 Now fold these new bottom corners up to meet the top corner.

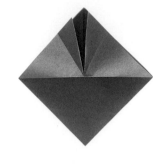

4 Next fold the front tips outwards.

5 Fold up the bottom corner of the top layer, as illustrated above.

6 Next fold up the edge of this new flap.

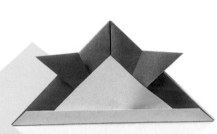

7 Fold up the remaining flap and tuck it inside.

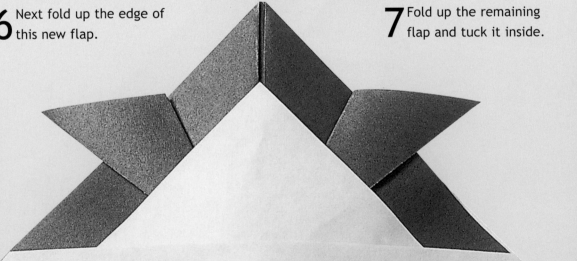

Pencil

You can make a whole set of coloured pencils to display using this fun and simple design. This model uses a rectangle four times longer than its width (4 x 1). For a longer pencil, use 6 x 1 or 8 x 1 paper.

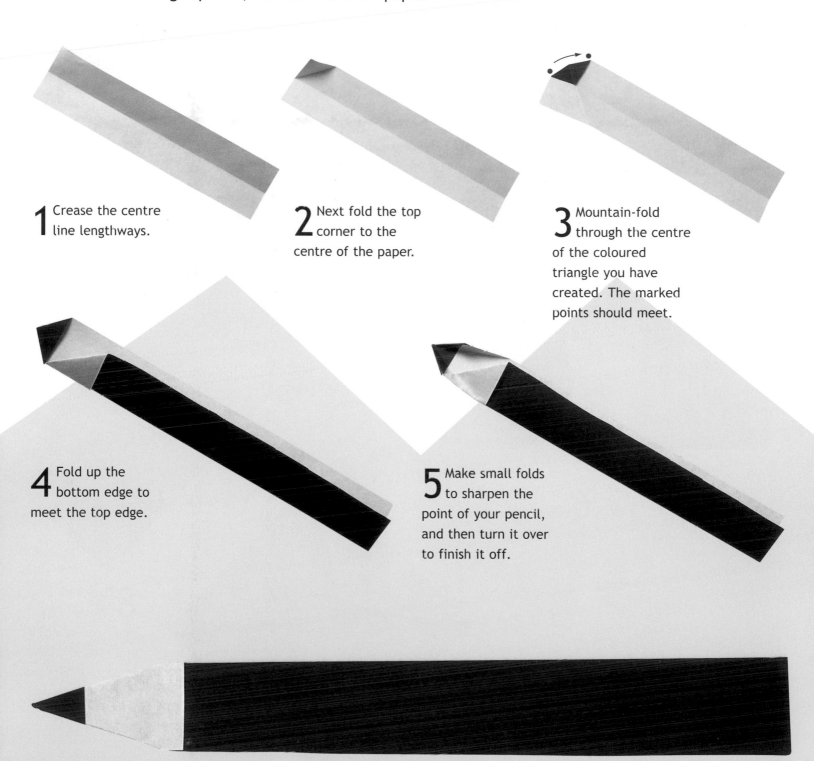

1 Crease the centre line lengthways.

2 Next fold the top corner to the centre of the paper.

3 Mountain-fold through the centre of the coloured triangle you have created. The marked points should meet.

4 Fold up the bottom edge to meet the top edge.

5 Make small folds to sharpen the point of your pencil, and then turn it over to finish it off.

Yakko-san

Another traditional design from Japan, this can be decorated with a face if you wish. It may be a good idea to use larger-sized paper for this model.

1 Crease both the horizontal and the vertical centre lines.

2 Fold all four corners into the centre.

3 This creates the first blintz base.

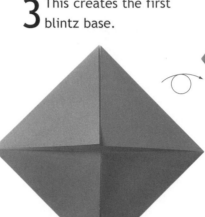

4 Turn the paper over. Fold all four corners into the centre again.

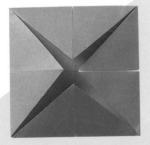

5 This creates the second blintz base.

6 Turn over. Fold the four corners into the centre once more.

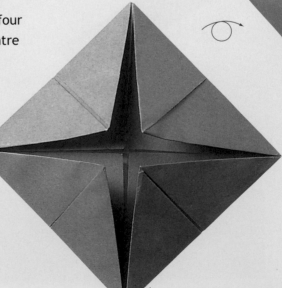

7 This creates a third and final blintz.

8 Turn over. Now fold the inner corner out and return.

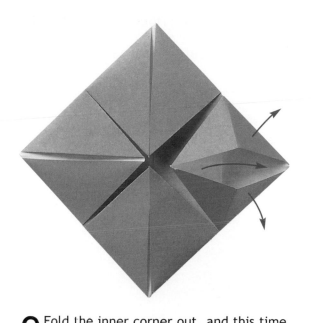

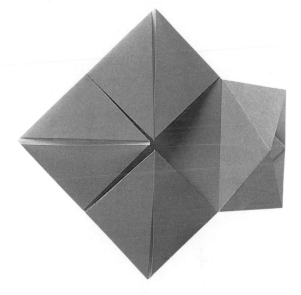

9 Fold the inner corner out, and this time pull out the coloured triangles.

10 Repeat steps 8 and 9 on two more corners to complete the model.

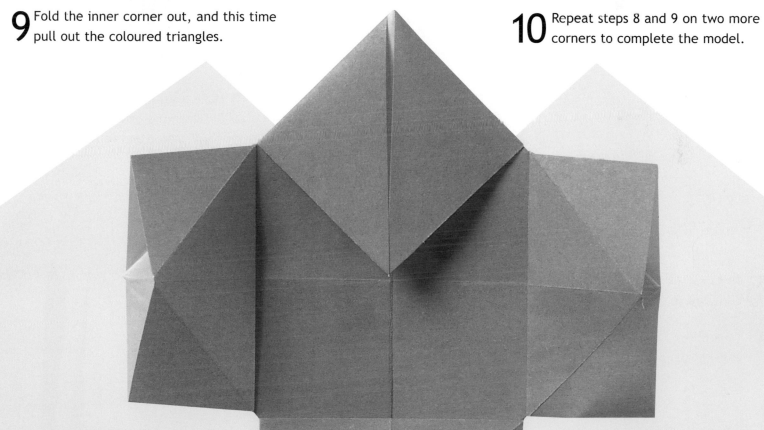

Japanese lady

This is a pretty model that can be adapted to create any number of figures. The model is made in two stages: the kimono and the head. Using special patterned paper can provide a particularly appealing effect.

kimono

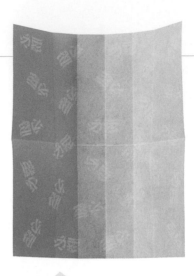

1 Crease both the horizontal and the vertical centre lines.

2 Fold both the left-hand and the right-hand edges into the centre and return.

3 Make a valley fold halfway between the centre crease and the left-hand crease and return. Repeat on the right-hand side.

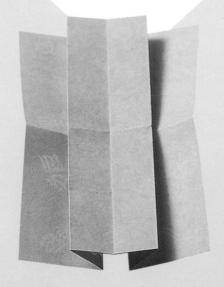

4 Pleat to the centre along these creases. The outer creases should be valley folds, while the inner creases are mountain folds.

5 Fold the model in half from front to back using a mountain fold.

6 Fold the front layer on both sides to the centre and then squash the top corners.

7 Mountain-fold the back flap upwards along the line of the bottom of the white triangles.

8 Your model should now look like this. Turn it over.

9 Swivel the flaps down. There should be a valley crease in the white underlayer.

10 This is your completed kimono.

head

1 This begins with a square, folded diagonally. The paper size is half that for the kimono. Fold again diagonally and then return.

2 Fold the top corner down by approximately one-quarter of the length of the paper.

3 Fold in the top edges. The top corners lie on the side of the coloured triangle.

4 This is the result. Now turn the model over.

5 Fold both sides to the centre line.

6 Now turn your model over once more.

7 This is the completed head. Combine it with the kimono for the finished model.

Beating heart 1 .... novelty models ◆

This is a fun moving model that makes a heartbeat sound when pressed. You will need a 4 x 1 rectangle and should begin with the coloured side face up.

1 Fold the strip of paper vertically in half.

2 Fold down the top folded corner to meet the bottom edge.

3 Squash this fold. (For instructions on squash-folding, see page 11.)

4 Petal-fold the squash you have just made. (See page 12 for full petal-fold instructions.)

5 Fold in the left-hand corners of the top layer. Repeat at the rear.

6 Now separate the layers of paper.

7 This shows the rear of the model.

8 Grasp the tab at the rear between your finger and thumb. Push into the centre of the petal fold with your thumbnail. The heart will beat. Relax your thumb to reset it.

Football strip

This is a fun design based on a traditional model. You can use any coloured paper you like to create shirts and shorts in your own team's colours. It consists of two models: a shirt and shorts. The shirt requires a rectangle of paper twice as long as it is wide. The shorts require a square, which may need to be trimmed to fit.

shirt

1 Crease the rectangle into quarters vertically. Valley-fold the two bottom corners and then fold a small strip at the top to the rear.

2 Crease and return the bottom corners and then fold the sides into the centre.

3 Fold the top to the rear. Fold the bottom to the rear and return.

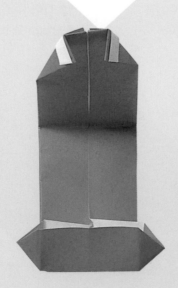

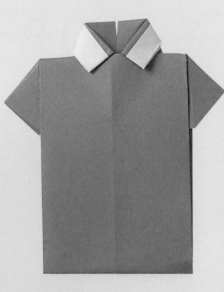

4 Pull out the bottom flaps. Fold the top corners to the middle.

5 Fold up the bottom to the top, tucking the edge under the collar tips.

6 This is your completed shirt.

shorts

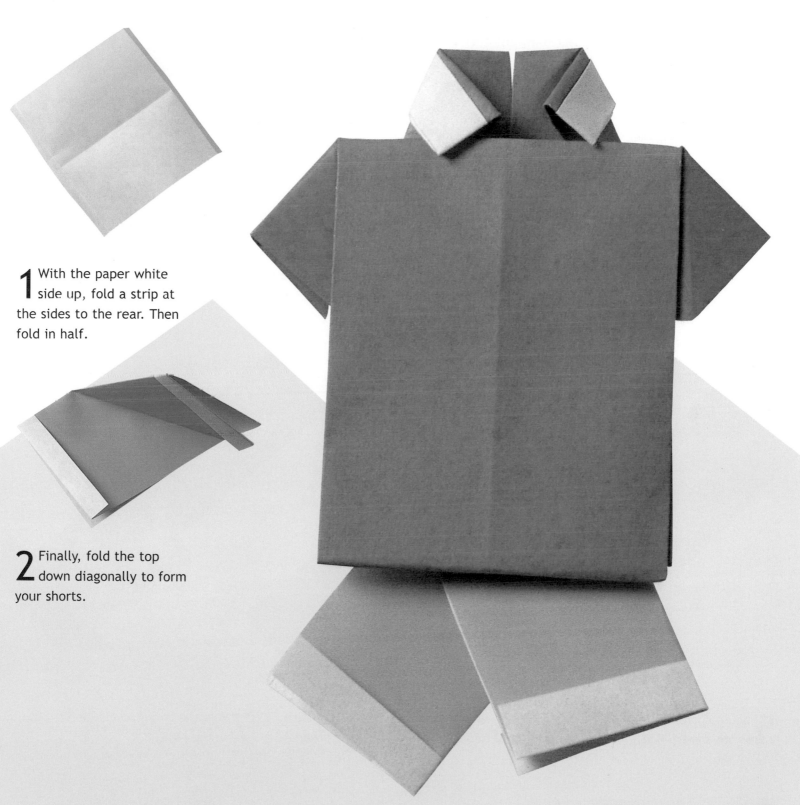

1 With the paper white side up, fold a strip at the sides to the rear. Then fold in half.

2 Finally, fold the top down diagonally to form your shorts.

Paintbrush

This is a relatively simple model, but care must be taken to make the folds accurate.

The model requires a strip of 4 x 1 paper. It begins with the coloured side face up.

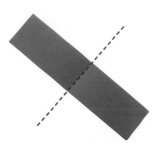

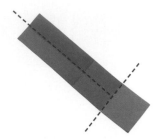

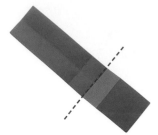

1 First crease a vertical centre line.

2 To the left of this centre line, fold and return a horizontal centre line. To the right of the original centre line, fold and return another vertical centre line.

3 Between the two vertical centre lines, fold and return a further vertical centre line.

4 Pleat the right-hand edge to the centre crease created in step 3.

5 Mountain-fold this edge to the rear on the centre line.

6 Mountain-fold the top and bottom edges inside. Squash the corners.

7 Fold the long flap at the left out to the right.

8 Fold the right-hand edge to meet the imaginary line formed between the inside corners of the main shape.

9 Fold the long sides to the centre and squash the left-hand corners.

10 Round the handle of the brush by blunting the corners. Fold in the top and bottom edges of the brush head.

Page markers ....

Once you have mastered the art of making the page-marker base, you can create a variety of different figures — just use your imagination. Here we show two examples. The page-marker base requires a strip of 4 x 1 paper.

page-marker base

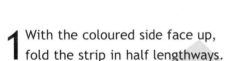

1 With the coloured side face up, fold the strip in half lengthways.

2 Fold the top layer vertically and squash the top right-hand corner.

3 This is the result that you should end up with.

4 Turn the model over. Once again, fold the top layer vertically and squash the top right-hand corner.

5 Fold the edges to the centre and return. Repeat at the rear. Return the edges to the centre and inside reverse-fold the four corners.

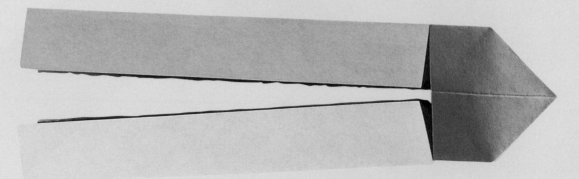

6 Fold the bottom strip to the top. Turn over and repeat at the rear. This is called a book fold.

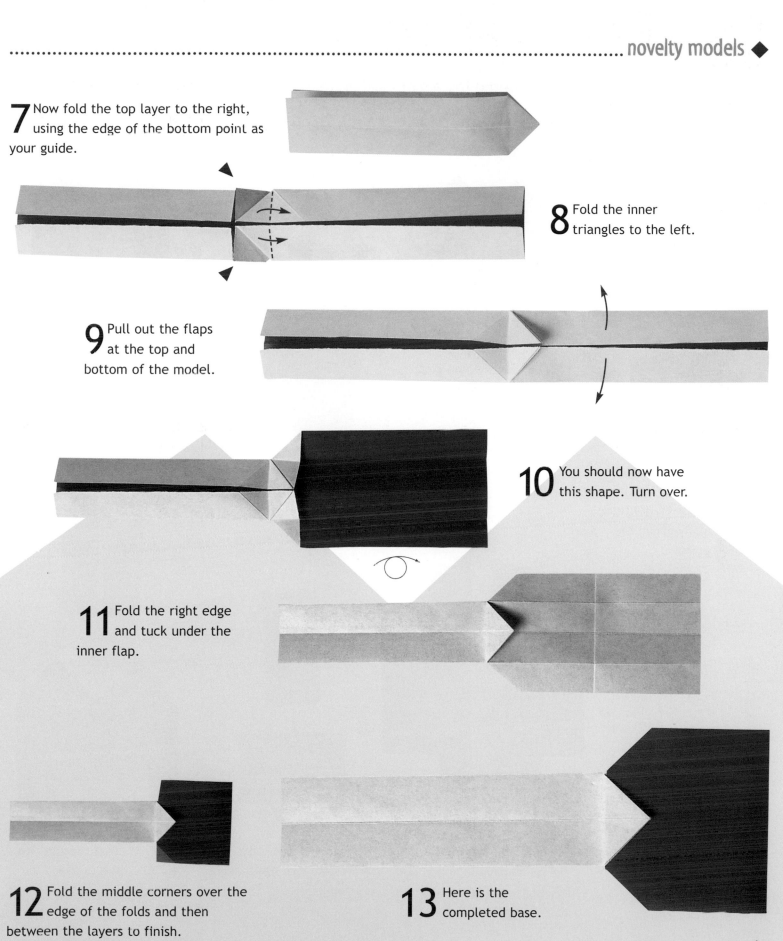

7 Now fold the top layer to the right, using the edge of the bottom point as your guide.

8 Fold the inner triangles to the left.

9 Pull out the flaps at the top and bottom of the model.

10 You should now have this shape. Turn over.

11 Fold the right edge and tuck under the inner flap.

12 Fold the middle corners over the edge of the folds and then between the layers to finish.

13 Here is the completed base.

Santa page marker

1 Begin with the page-marker base. Fold the top of the base to the rear, folding slightly above the coloured points.

2 Fold out the flap and squash the corners at the top.

3 Fold up a short strip at the bottom.

4 This is the result you should end up with.

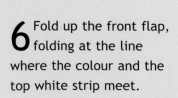

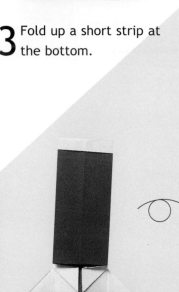

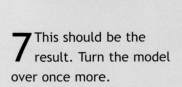

5 Turn the model over and then fold the sides to the centre.

6 Fold up the front flap, folding at the line where the colour and the top white strip meet.

7 This should be the result. Turn the model over once more.

8 Fold down the top flap so that it overlaps the white edge in the middle.

9 Tuck the top edge of the white centre shape inside the white edge you have just folded down. (You may find it easier to fold in the top corners of the strip to be tucked in).

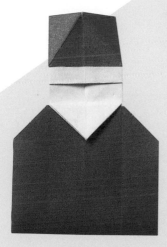

10 Fold the top corners behind the model to complete Santa's hat.

nurse page marker

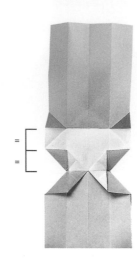

1 Start with a page-marker base, with the colour reversed.

2 Fold under the bottom tip of the coloured band. Turn the model over.

3 Fold out the flaps at the top and squash the corners at the bottom.

4 Fold the top flap down and the sides in.

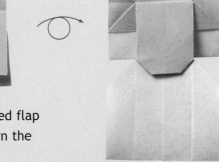

5 Fold the coloured flap up and then turn the model over again.

6 Fold the top down and the sides in.

7 Fold the side flaps down and then tuck them inside to finish the model.

Robin Hood/airman............... novelty models ◆

Something for the children; start with the page marker base and follow simple steps to create your own Robin of Sherwood.

Start — page-marker base

1 Fold top to rear.

2 Fold flaps back. Turn over.

3 Fold flap up.

4 Inside, reverse top corner, then fold top part to rear. Turn over.

5 Tuck top of head inside top flap.

6 Inside reverse. Turn over.

7 Tuck corner inside. Turn over.

Chef

To get the colour of "Chefs Whites" reverse the paper with the page marker base.

A truly lovely present for cooks everywhere.

Start — page-marker base

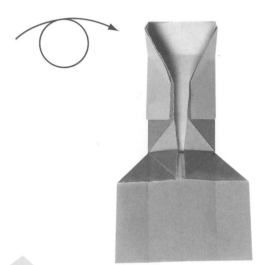

1 Tuck tip of chin under, peel top down, and turn over.

2 Pull corners out.

3 Result. Turn over.

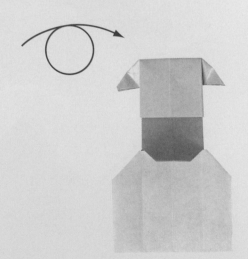

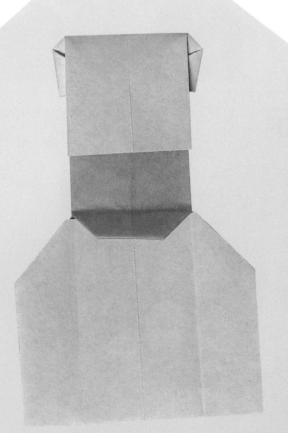

4 Tuck corners between layers.

Eccentric page-marker base............

A kooky page-marker base, but hey — great fun to fold and make.

1 4 x 1 fold where indicated.

2 Fold long edges together. Fold top layer back, squash bottom corner.

3 Fold behind bottom layer. Squash bottom corner.

4 Fold edges to centre and return, also at back. Fold edges to centre and inside reverse fold at corners.

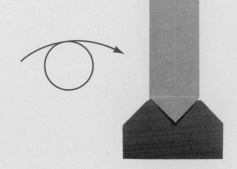

5 Bookfold.

6 Fold tip up.

7 Fold flaps out.

8 Fold flap back, end meets top of white triangles.

9 Fold corner between layers.

10 Result. Turn over.

11 Base complete.

The whole man

Start — eccentric pagemarker base.

1 Fold tip under.

2 Result, turn over.

3 Open out top flaps and squash at bottom.

4 Fold top down and corners inside.

5 Fold sides to centre.

6 Crimp to form ears.

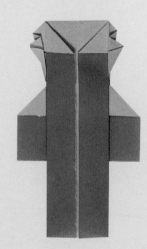

7 Result, turn over.

Rocking Santa .... novelty models ◆

A festive model that makes an ideal Christmas decoration, particularly if you make several. This model begins with a square sheet folded diagonally through the centre and with the coloured side face up.

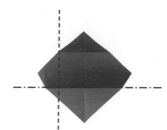

1 Crease a diagonal line, pinch it at the centre and return. Fold the right-hand corner to the centre and then return.

2 Fold the left-hand corner to the crease. Mountain-fold the top and bottom corners to the rear.

3 Mountain-fold the model horizontally in half.

4 Squash the top right-hand corner.

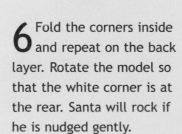

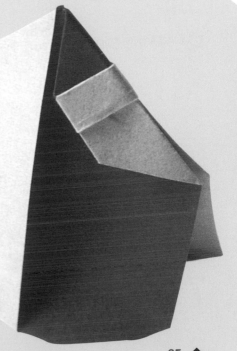

5 Fold the bottom corner of the top layer inside. Repeat at the rear. Fold the flap of the squashed fold back on itself several times. This forms Santa's hatband.

6 Fold the corners inside and repeat on the back layer. Rotate the model so that the white corner is at the rear. Santa will rock if he is nudged gently.

Chinaman page marker

This is a fun model to fold and a great page marker into the bargain.

1 4 x 1 crease centre. Fold top quarter to rear.

2 Form waterbomb double thickness.

3 Fold flap up.

4 Fold down at half height of waterbomb.

5 Fold sides in, squash at corners.

6 Push sides in, then fold to bottom.

6a Partway tuck top part inside waterbomb.

6b Fold flaps down.

7 Open out lower flaps.

8 Result. Turn over when complete. Page corner fits under here.

9 Fold edge under chin. Tuck corners between layers.

10 This Chinaman sits on the corner of the page to remind me of the place to resume my reading.

Pen .... novelty models ◆

Using a waterbomb base in this model, start with some foil and create your very own personal ink pen.

Use 4x1 strip — foil is good.

1 Crease diagonals.

2 Fold corners to centre point.

3 Form a waterbomb base.

4 Fold sides to centre point, then fold strip back.

5 Sink point.

6 Valley fold corners to centreline.

7 Fold folded edges to centreline, then turn over.

8 Mountain fold top tip inside and lower edge behind, then turn over.

9 Curl and interlock.

If made from foil, this model does write when dipped in real ink. The split in the paper acts as an ink reservoir.

English Policeman

The model begins with a complicated base which will require plenty of practice.

Start — portrait base, inverted

1 Raise back layer.

2 Fold top edges to centreline.

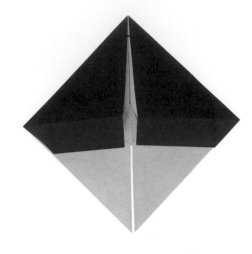

3 Fold flaps under.

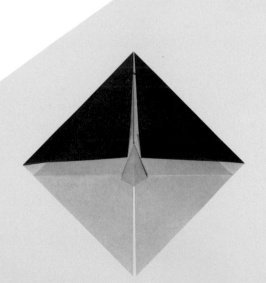

4 Tuck flaps under nose.

5 Result. Turn over.

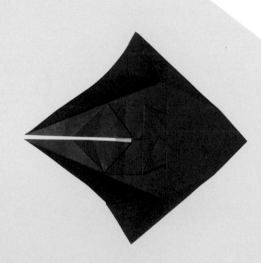

6 These edges fold to touch the edges of the central flaps.

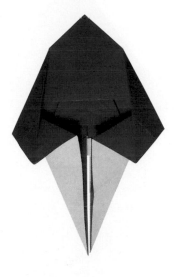

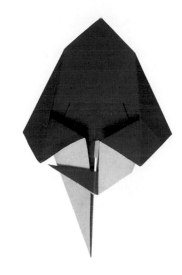

7 Inside reverse flap.

8 Mountain fold between split.

9 Result. Repeat steps 7 & 8 on other flap.

10 Result. Turn over.

Christmas lantern

This pretty three-dimensional model makes an excellent tree decoration. It is another complex model, so will require both practice and patience. This begins with the preliminary base, closed end down.

1 Crease and return the top corner to meet the bottom corner, but do not fold. Make a pinch only. Fold and return the bottom corner to the pinch. Sink the bottom corner (for sink instructions, see page 19).

2 Fold both the left- and right-hand corners to the centre line and return. Repeat at the rear.

3 Sink each of these four corners.

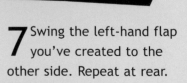

4 Fold the left point to the top point, crease and return. Fold the left point to the bottom point, crease and return. Repeat at the rear. Do the same on the hidden side flaps.

5 Fold down the top corner to the front, creasing along an imaginary line between the left- and right-hand corners. Repeat at rear. Do the same on the hidden side flaps.

6 Collapse the left- and right-hand flaps inwards, using the existing creases. Repeat at the rear and also on the hidden side flaps.

7 Swing the left-hand flap you've created to the other side. Repeat at rear.

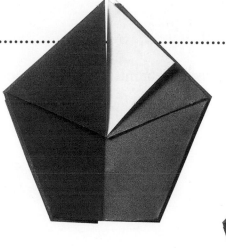

8 Fold the flap back along the centre line.

9 Tuck the flap inside the pocket created in the coloured section. Repeat at the rear.

10 Swing the remaining flap to the left. Now repeat at the rear.

11 Tuck this flap inside the right-hand coloured pocket. Repeat at the rear. Perform steps 7–11 on the hidden side flaps.

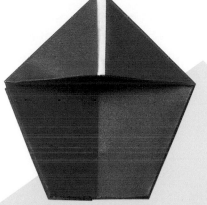

12 Tuck under the middle flap, using a mountain fold. Repeat at the rear.

13 Pull up the four flaps at the top. Insert a finger into the base to manoeuvre the model into three dimensions and complete it.

3D heart

This is an attractive model that can be made into a pretty handmade pop-up card containing a special note. The card itself can be made from any type of coloured card of your choice.

1 Crease both horizontal and vertical centre lines and return.

2 Valley-fold the left- and right-hand corners to the centre and return. Mountain-fold the bottom corner to the rear and then return again.

3 Crease the sheet into quarters. Do this by folding each of the edges to the centre line. Return after folding.

4 Crease the top corner to meet the bottom crease and return. Crease the bottom corner upwards to meet the bottom crease and return.

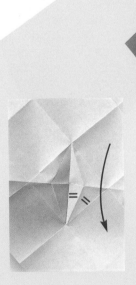

5 Crease two valleys and one mountain in the central top diamond, as illustrated, then fold.

6 The model is three-dimensional and concave on this side. Inside reverse-fold the top corners.

7 Inside reverse-fold the top corners. The fold should begin from the centre of the square edge.

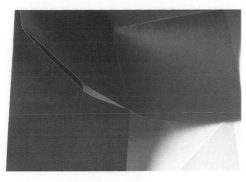

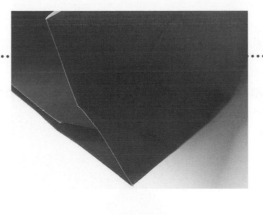

8 Make folds as shown to tuck the outer edges into the model.

9 The tucking fold at the top can be tricky. Valley-fold the left-hand edge along the inner edge.

10 Now fold in this corner along the inner edge and return.

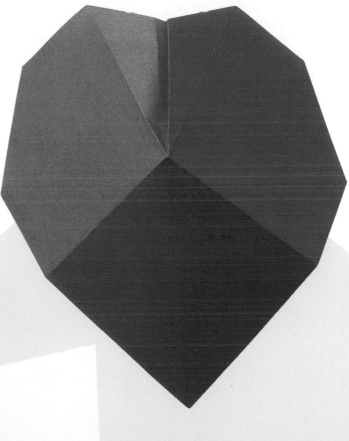

11 Using the crease lines you have created, tuck the corner into the top pocket.

12 Tuck the top layer of the bottom corner into the pocket behind.

13 You can now slide a personalised note into this inner pocket if you wish. Turn the model over for the 3D heart.

14 You can also use the heart as a basis for a romantic card.

Lighthouse

White side up this model begins with a waterbomb base, resulting in a very neat and useful bookmark.

1 Fold diagonals, then horizontal crease, and finally collapse into waterbomb base.

2 Fold points to top point.

3 Squash both flaps.

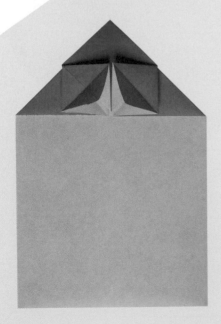

4 Fold top triangle, both sides.

5 Fold edges back to centre.

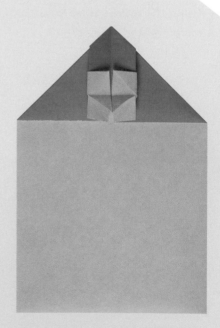

6 Fold triangle up.

7 Pull out corners.

8 Fold up strip twice as wide as top strip.

9 Fold strip in half.

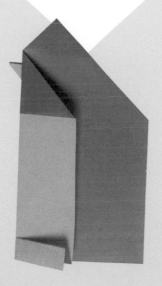

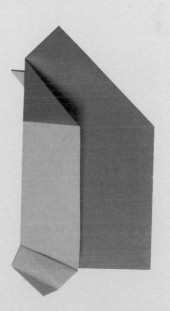

10 Fold edge to back, fold passes approximately halfway along top white triangle. Turn model over.

11 Pull down concertina edge and flatten.

12 Fold edge to line up with coloured edge.

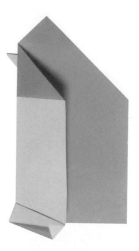

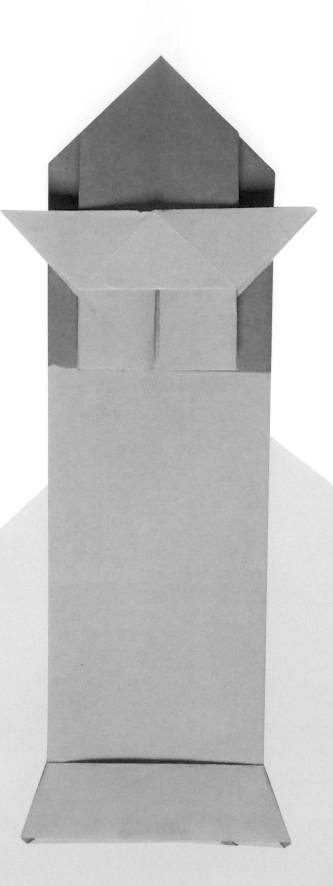

13 Fold edge to line up with coloured edge.

14 Fold edge to line up with coloured edge and repeat in mirror image steps 11,12,13. Finally, tuck right flap into left flap white triangle to lock.

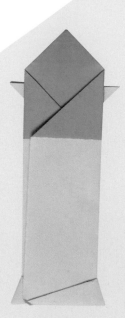

15 Result. Turn over.

difficulty :

origin :
david petty

Space rocket

Great to make with children. Let them watch as the rocket unfolds before their eyes.

1 Crease thirds.

2 Crease centreline.

3 Fold corners to centreline.

4 Fold on thirds line.

5 Fold edge to outer edge and return.

6 Fold crease to outer edge.

7 Result. Repeat steps 4-7 on left-hand side.

8 Result. Open side flaps and convert to reverse folds.

9 Fold lower edge so it overlaps the coloured paper.

 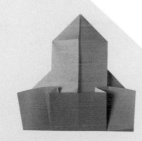

10 Pull out side flaps.

11 Tuck tips inside.

 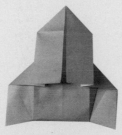 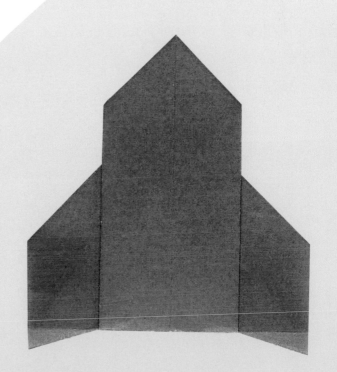

12 Tuck flap under.

13 Result of tuck-in. Turn over.

Kettle

This traditional model begins with a waterbomb base and will need to be inflated to 3D.
It really is quite unique and will operate as a kettle, using a candle as a heater BUT
ONLY under adult supervision!

1 Form waterbomb base.

2 Fold tip to bottom point.

3 Fold corner to centre.

4 Unfold to step 2.

5 Fold using existing creases.

6 Fold flap across.

7 Result. Repeat on the other three flaps.

8 Result. Inflate to 3D model.

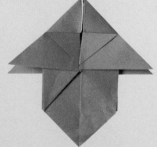

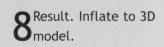

This will operate as a kettle using a candle as heater BUT
ONLY under adult supervision!

Olympian love

The Olympian god's couldn't have made a better job of piercing a lover's heart.

1 Crease quarters. Pleat.

2 Fold corners to centreline.

3 Fold right edge to coloured edge and return, then turn over.

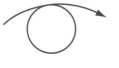

4 Crease top corners and fold lower flap down.

5 Inside reverse left corners. Valley fold right flap.

6 Make folds then open out fully.

7 Precrease.

8 Precrease.

9 Precrease at top. Valley lower edge.

10 Fold in half.

11 Make crease, then open fully.

  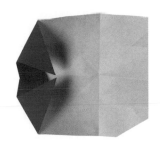 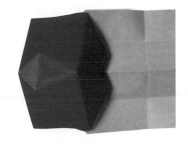

12 Fold up lower edge, putting in folds on existing creases. Bottom part is 3D from here on.

13 Squash corners.

14 Fold lower portion up.

15 Mountain fold corners.

16 Fold corners in and pleat.

17 Inside reverse corners then fold point down.

18 Fold top down and turn over.

19 Fold sides to centre. Rotate.

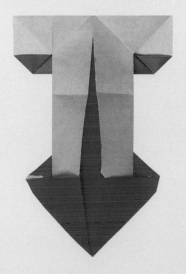 

20 Fold top inside. Valley fold points and turn over.

Bells

These bells would complement a greetings card in celebration of a forthcoming marriage.

Start — preliminary base

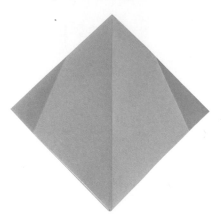

1 Fold so folded edge is parallel to centreline.

2 Unfold corners, tuck one between layers.

3 Slide/rotate sideways. The sideways motion is limited by a hidden flap.

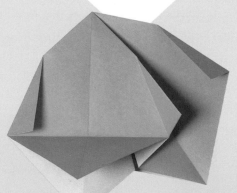

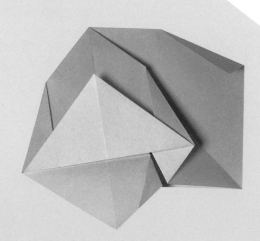

4 First, refold side corners, then tuck the tip inside and turn over.

5 Refold the corner, then fold tip up.

6 Tuck tip inside, squash on right.

7 Tuck tip inside, leaving point as clapper.

8 Swing flap across.

9 Tuck tip inside, leaving point as clapper.

10 Blunt points. Tuck in white triangle.

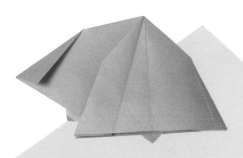

11 Turn over.

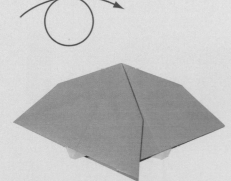

12 Complete.

Turkish slippers

This model will amaze and delight as the paper transforms itself into delicate slippers.

1 Fold sides in.

2 Waterbomb one end.

3 Crease centre and return. Squash waterbomb flaps and return.

4 Reverse fold side, repeat at top.

5 Partially open out and turn over.

6 Collapse, then turn over.

7 Tuck tips inside.

8 Tuck in one section, one side only.

9 Bring paper across and down, one side only. Fold tip behind.

10 Tuck tip under layer behind.

11 Raise rear portion.

12 Fold sides flat to rear.

13 Fold flap down.

14 Showing creases.

15 Tuck flap inside triangular pockets.

16 Reverse fold corners and round back.

Complete.
Make the other half of the pair from the remainder of the sheet.

Buffet server

To complement any party, this is the perfect way to organise cutlery.

1 Fold in half.

2 Fold in half, rotate so 4 corners are at the top.

3 Fold top layer down.

4 Fold top layer down.

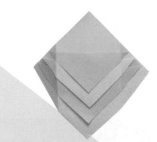

5 Fold top layer down.

6 Fold sides to rear — they will overlap.

7 Complete.

Church

An ideal first model for beginners starting with a waterbomb base,

it quickly transforms into a completed church.

1 Form waterbomb base.

2 Valley fold points to top point.

3 Mountain fold points to top point and repeat at back.

4 Squash front flaps.

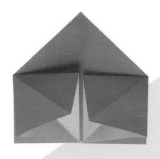

5 Squash rear flaps.

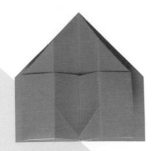

6 Mountain fold sides behind centre.

7 Lift front layer and squash.

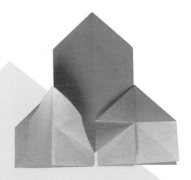

8 Repeat squashes at rear.

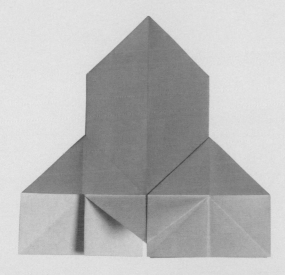

9 Fold up flap, repeat at rear.

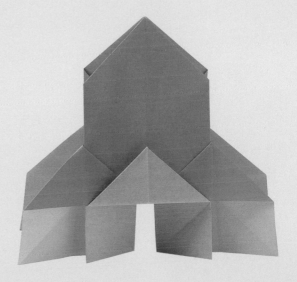

10 Complete.

difficulty :

origin :
traditional

Lantern

A beautiful paper lantern what could be simpler.

1 Crease halfway lines, fold sides to middle.

2 Fold corners in.

3 Result. Turn over.

4 Fold points to centre.

5 Result. Turn over.

6 Fold corners in about a third of the way.

7 Result. Turn over.

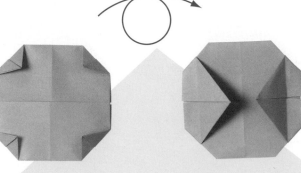

8 Valley fold points out.

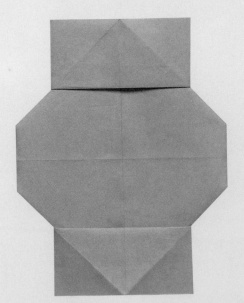

Cowboy hat

Every budding young cowboy will want one of these, great fun to make and enjoy.

1 Fold diagonal.

2 Pinch bisector at edge.

3 Fold corner to pinch.

4 Fold corner to point.

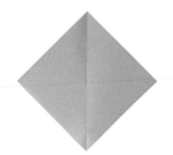

5 Fold corner up.

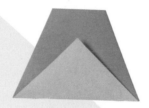

6 Fold corner up.

7 Put fingers inside and separate layers, flatten, and push top inside.

8 Fold front and back points up.

9 Pull out points.

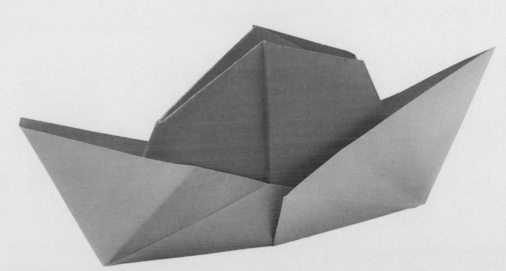

Composite doll

This is quite an exquisite model. Made in four parts with clear and easy-to-follow steps; turn your doll into a lady or chorister in a church choir.

Head

1 Crease centre, fold 1/6 down.

2 Fold sides to centre.

3 Resut. Turn over.

4 Fold sides to centre — allow paper at rear to flip to front.

5 Result. Turn over.

6 Fold sides to folded edge.

7 Pleat.

8 Fold lower sides to rear, squash small triangles.

9 Fold corners to rear.

10 Fold corners to lock, then turn over.

11 Folds.

12 Complete.

Lower part

1 Pleat central eighths.

2 Mountain fold in half.

3 Pull top layers sideways, flatten at top.

4 Result, turn over.

5 Fold flap up.

6 Fold sides in, squash at sides.

7 Result. Turn over.

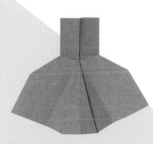

8 Complete.

Upper part

As lower body to step 5, then . . .

6a Fold sides to centre, squash at top.

7a Result. Turn over.

8a Complete.

Assembly insert rear flaps into pockets

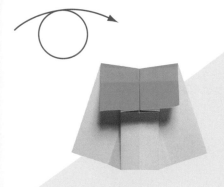   

1 Pleat central eighths.

2 Mountain fold in top third.

3 Pull top layer sideways.

4 Result. Turn over.

  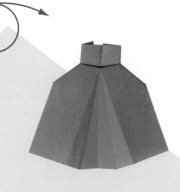

5 Fold flap up.

6 Fold sides in, squash at sides.

7 Result. Turn over.

8 Complete.

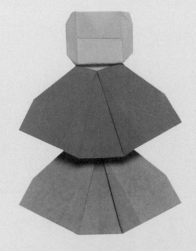 

Lady

Assemble by tucking rear flaps into pockets.

Chorister

Candle .... novelty models ◆

A lovely festive model; why not make a few for a Christmas centre piece.

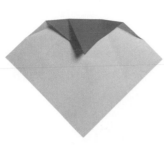

1 Fold one corner to centre.

2 Fold sides of triangle under and top edges down.

3 Result. Turn over.

4 Fold corners to centre.

5 Fold flap down. Allow point at back to flip.

6 Fold sides in, tuck one inside the other.

7 Fold up bottom triangle, turn over.

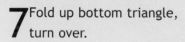

difficulty :

origin :
david petty

Heart page maker

Why not try this romantic version of a page marker. A simple model with clear step-by-step guides; a great way to mark your page and a wonderful way of showing how much you care.

1 Fold and return.

2 Fold lower corners to centre.

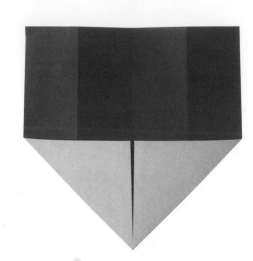

3 Fold to centreline, top part only.

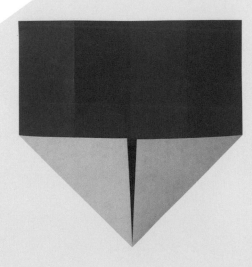

4 Fold and return, between vertical creases, halfway to white edge.

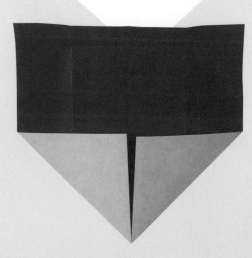

5 Fold and return, between vertical creases, halfway to crease in step 4.

6 Fold and return to form cross between vertical creases. Turn over.

7 Fold and return.

8 Collapse.

9 Fold edge down, squash corners.

10 Fold top corners in.

11 Raise lower flap and pull sides out. Fold points in.

12 Fold corners inside.

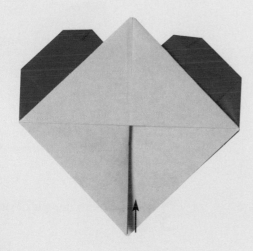 

13 Page corner fits here. Turn over.

Finished heart on page.

difficulty :

origin :

traditional

Star

MAKING AN EQUILATERAL TRIANGLE FROM A RECTANGLE.

Newspaper can be used.

1 Crease in centre.

2 Fold corner to crease, fold starts at bottom corner.

3 Fold along edge of folded triangle.

4 Tuck triangle inside. Equilateral triangle complete. Turn over to plain side to make star.

MAKING THE STAR

Start with side without edges on top.

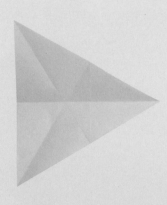

1 Crease centrelines.

2 Take each point to centre and return.

3 Take point to centre of opposite side.

  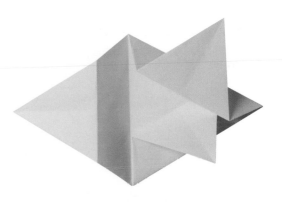

4 Fold out point on existing crease.

5 Repeat steps 3 and 4 on next point.

6 Repeat steps 3 and 4 on the next point.

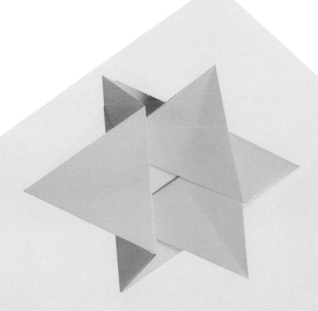 

7 Bring layer underneath to front.

Pagoda

A traditional model of a resplendent pagoda or tiered tower, of intermediate difficulty it begins with a waterbomb base.

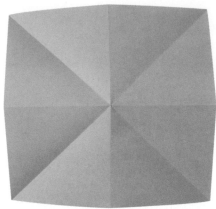

1 Form waterbomb base.

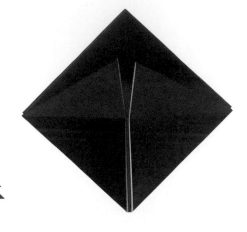

2 Fold corners to top point. Repeat at back.

3 Fold corners to bottom point and return. Repeat at back.

4 Open each flap and squash.

5 Fold top layer only.

6 Fold sides behind to centre.

7 Fold point up.

8 Pull out corners.

9 Unit complete.

Assembly

A Slide top unit onto lower unit, and tuck the flaps into the pockets of the lower unit.

For best effect, fold units from successively reduced size paper — reducing by 6mm (1/4 in) each time.

◆4 modular designs

These models are particularly fun to make, and with a little experimentation with folds and use of colour you can create your own variations.

difficulty :

origin :
david petty

Napkin ring

A simple way to make unusual table decorations. You need to make five modules.

Choose your colours and paper patterns to match the occasion.

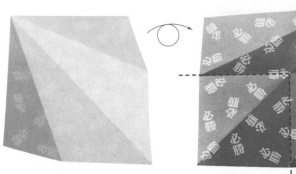

1 First crease a diagonal centre line. Crease and return to edges to the centre and return.

2 Turn the sheet over. Crease the top left-hand corner from the left edge to the central crease and return. Repeat for the bottom right-hand corner.

3 Raise the lower left-hand corner and bring the sides together. Fold down the sides at an angle, front and back.

4 Tuck both the back and front tips between the layers of paper.

5 This step creates your first module.

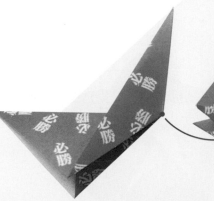

6 To join, tuck the flaps at the rear of the right-hand module into the pockets of the left-hand module so that the marked points meet.

7 Fold down the top flap and tuck it inside. The marked points should meet.

8 This picture shows two modules joined together. Join the other modules in the same way.

9 The model must be pulled into three dimensions to make the last join. It can either be concave or convex. The front is convex in this photograph.

10 The back of the napkin ring is seen as concave in this photograph.

Simple star

This is an easy model, which consists of four identical modules. They are ideal as decorations or for adding the finishing touch to wrapped presents, particularly if they are made from foil paper.

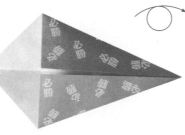

1 Crease a diagonal centre line. Fold in two corners so that they meet the centre line.

2 This makes the kite base. Now turn the model over.

3 Fold down the top edge so that the top left-hand corner meets the lower corner. The top right-hand corner should lie at the centre line.

4 Mountain-fold the new top left-hand corner behind, then return. This creates your module.

5 To join the modules, tuck the flap of one module inside the pocket of another.

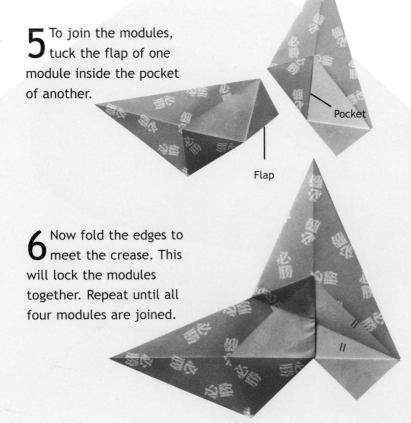

Pocket

Flap

6 Now fold the edges to meet the crease. This will lock the modules together. Repeat until all four modules are joined.

Christmas star

This is another festive model that makes an attractive Christmas decoration. It looks particularly nice when it is folded in foil, and there are several variations. You will need four modules with which to make it.

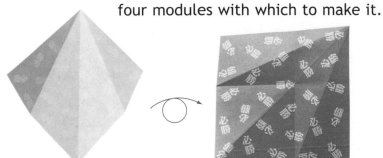 

1 First crease a diagonal centre line. Crease and return edges to the centre and return.

2 Turn the sheet over. Crease the top left-hand corner from the left edge to the central crease and return. Repeat for the bottom right-hand corner. Raise the lower left-hand corner and then bring the sides together.

3 Fold down the sides, front and back. The crease runs from point to point.

4 Tuck both the back and front tips between the layers, folding over the layers behind.

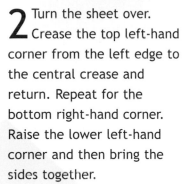

Pocket

Flap

5 Crease the top left-hand corner to the rear and return.

6 To join, tuck the flaps at the rear of the right-hand module into the rear pockets of the left-hand module. The top tip of the left-hand module should meet the tip of the right-hand module.

7 This photograph shows two joined modules. Join the remaining units in the same way.

8 Here are some variations that are easily made.

Hexagon puzzle

This is a fun puzzle that is surprisingly difficult to solve. We have used practice paper to make the first modules, but you will need to follow the colour scheme shown to complete the puzzle. You need six modules for each hexagon.

1 Fold the square in half vertically and return.

2 Take the bottom left-hand corner to a point along the vertical centre line just below the top edge (as marked) and return.

3 Now take the top left-hand corner to a point along the centre line just above the bottom edge (as marked) and return.

4 Fold in the left-hand edge. Fold from where the two creases meet.

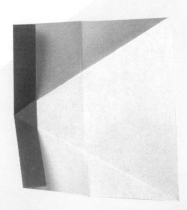

5 Fold down the top right-hand triangle using the existing creases. Fold up the bottom left-hand triangle, again using the existing creases.

6 Fold the bottom right-hand corner to meet the join on the top edge.

7 Tuck the triangle formed at top right inside the layers.

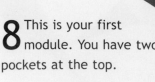

8 This is your first module. You have two pockets at the top.

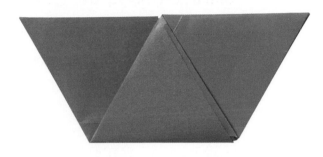

9 To join the modules, slide the point of the right-hand module into the pocket of the left-hand module.

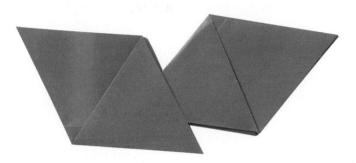

10 This photogrpah shows two modules joined together. Join the others in the same way.

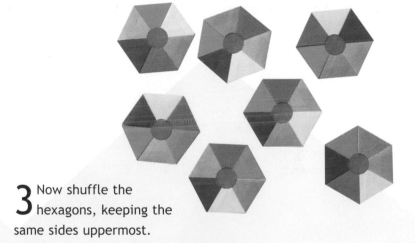

1 You will need seven hexagons for this puzzle. Paint a coloured dot on one side of each hexagon, or use a small sticker.

2 Use a different-coloured dot or sticker on the other side of each hexagon. If you get the sides confused after the hexagons have been mixed, you will never solve the puzzle!

3 Now shuffle the hexagons, keeping the same sides uppermost.

To complete the puzzle, you need to recreate the pattern shown in the diagram. However, touching colours must be the same. There is only one solution.

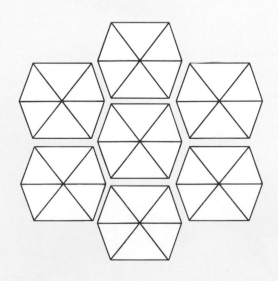

For the solution, see page 240

Millions-to-one

This is a decorative wreath that has a staggering 43,046,721 possible combinations. It would take nearly two years to fold them all — even without allowing time off to eat or sleep! You will need eight modules to create the wreath.

1 First fold a square sheet diagonally in half.

2 Fold the front edge to the bottom edge. Repeat at the rear.

3 Now you need to fold the front flap forwards.

4 Fold up the bottom right-hand corner so that it meets a point along the top edge.

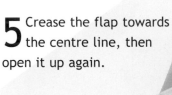

5 Crease the flap towards the centre line, then open it up again.

6 Now fold the top corner so that it meets a point along the bottom edge.

7 Crease the flap towards the centre line again and open it out.

8 Make a reverse fold at the right-hand side. Allow the small flaps inside to flip out.

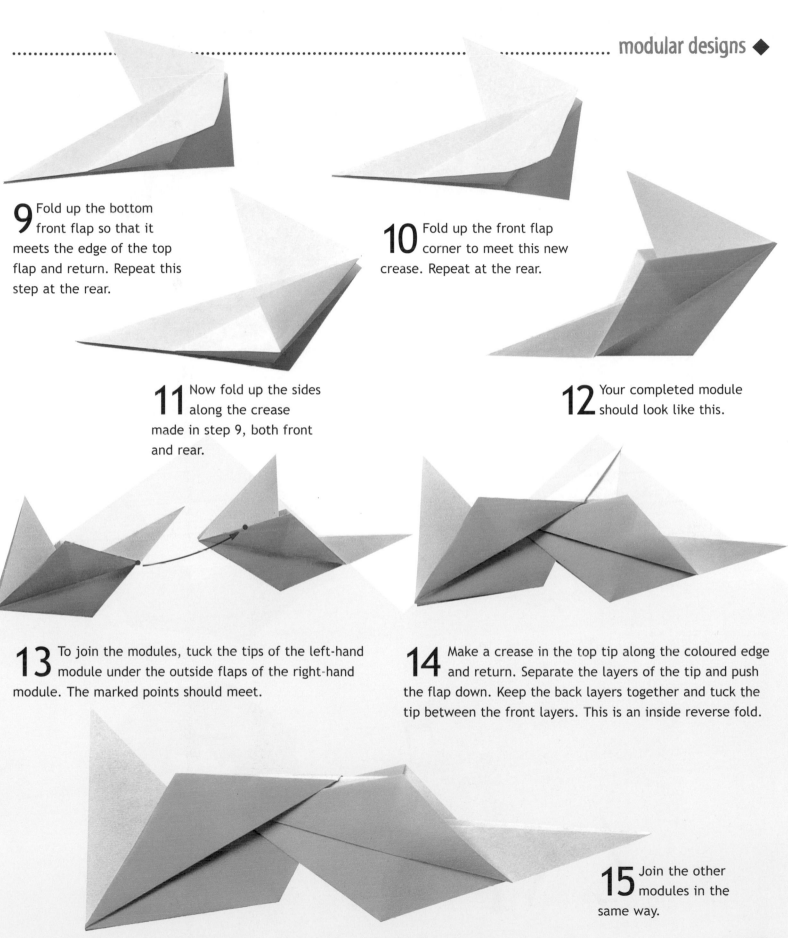

9 Fold up the bottom front flap so that it meets the edge of the top flap and return. Repeat this step at the rear.

10 Fold up the front flap corner to meet this new crease. Repeat at the rear.

11 Now fold up the sides along the crease made in step 9, both front and rear.

12 Your completed module should look like this.

13 To join the modules, tuck the tips of the left-hand module under the outside flaps of the right-hand module. The marked points should meet.

14 Make a crease in the top tip along the coloured edge and return. Separate the layers of the tip and push the flap down. Keep the back layers together and tuck the tip between the front layers. This is an inside reverse fold.

15 Join the other modules in the same way.

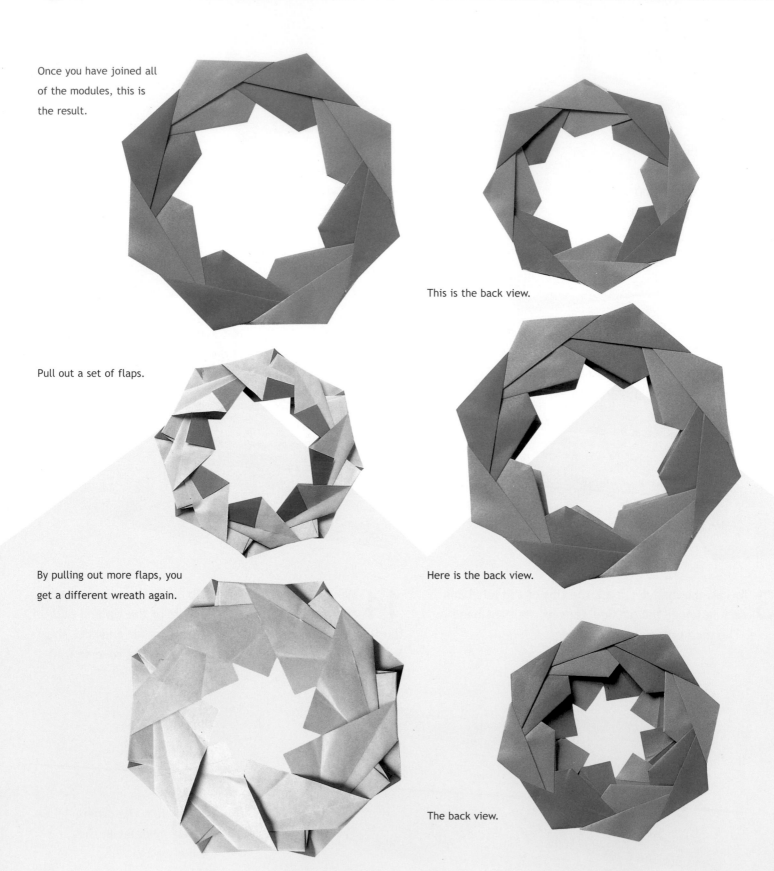

Once you have joined all
of the modules, this is
the result.

This is the back view.

Pull out a set of flaps.

Here is the back view.

By pulling out more flaps, you
get a different wreath again.

The back view.

Christmas wreath

This wreath can be made in different colours to suit different occasions and makes an unusual decoration. You will need to make nine modules.

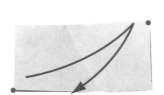

1 With the coloured side face up, fold a square of paper horizontally in half.

2 Fold up the bottom left-hand corner to meet the top right-hand corner and return. Make a reverse fold on the right-hand side.

3 Fold up the front flap to meet the top edge. Repeat at the rear.

4 Tuck the tips, front and back, between the central layers.

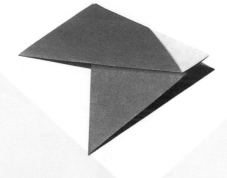

5 Now tuck the bottom flaps, both front and back, up between the central layers. The fold should run from corner to corner.

6 This completes your first module. You need nine in total.

7 To join the modules, tuck the bottom tips of the right-hand module between the layers at the front of the left-hand unit.

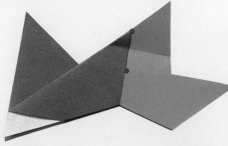
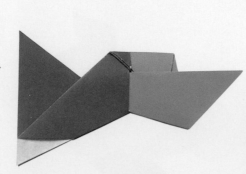
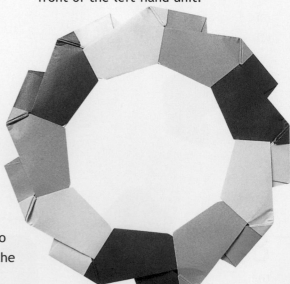

8 Tuck the top tip of the two joined units between the lower layers. The point where the white and the coloured paper join at the top edge should meet the corner of the top edge of the pocket.

9 This shows two modules joined correctly. Add the next module to the right-hand side and continue in the same way for the other modules.

Flower wheel .... modular designs ◆

This is a pretty example of the wheel pattern, which can be made using any mix of colours. However, the pattern of the paper is so delicate that it can be very effective in one colour. You will need 13 modules.

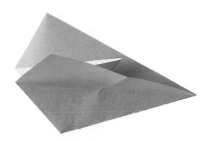

1 Take one edge of the paper to meet the opposite edge. Do not fold, only make a pinch.

2 Now fold the paper in half diagonally.

3 Fold the left-hand corner to meet the pinch on the right-hand edge. Now return. Make the creases into a reverse fold.

4 Now down fold the flaps, front and rear.

5 Tuck in the rear tips between the layers, folding them over the layer behind them.

6 This picture shows the completed module.

7 To join the modules, tuck the tips of the right-hand module into the pockets either side of the left-hand module. The marked points should meet.

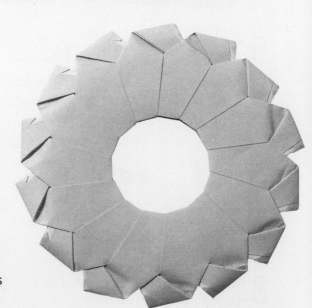

8 Fold the tip on the outside, lining up the marked points, then tuck the folded part between the layers.

9 This photograph shows two joined modules. Continue adding modules to the right.

The big wheel

There are a variety of different wheels that you can make, each using slightly different modules. Here we will look at two examples of wheels. Again, the colours can be combined in any way you wish.

wheel 1 ◆ Use 7cm paper to give you a 25cm diameter wheel. You will need 24 modules.

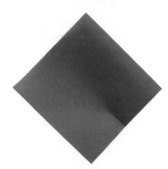
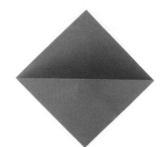

1 With the coloured side face up, take one edge of the paper to meet the opposite edge. Do not fold, only make a pinch.

2 Now fold the paper in half diagonally.

3 Fold the left-hand corner to meet the pinch on the right-hand edge. Now return. Make a reverse fold at the left-hand corner.

4 Now fold down the flaps, front and rear.

5 Tuck in the rear tips between the layers.

6 This is the completed module. It is the same as the module for the flower wheel on page 133, but the assembly of the wheel is different.

7 Tuck the tips of the right-hand module into the pockets of the left-hand module. The points marked on the photographs should meet.

8 Tuck the tip into the pocket. The marked points should meet.

9 Here are two joined modules. Join the others from the right.

wheel 2 ◆ Use 7cm paper to give you a 22cm diameter wheel. You will need 22 modules.

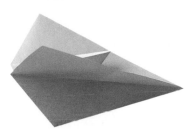

1 With the coloured side face up, take one edge of the paper to the opposite edge. Do not fold, only make a pinch.

2 Now fold the paper in half diagonally.

3 Fold the left-hand corner to meet the pinch on the right-hand edge. Now return. Make a reverse fold at the left-hand corner.

4 Now fold down the flaps, front and rear, and return.

5 Fold down the sides so that the top edge meets the left-hand edge. Repeat at the rear.

6 Fold down the sides. Repeat at the rear. This completes the module.

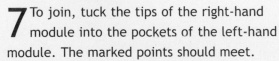

7 To join, tuck the tips of the right-hand module into the pockets of the left-hand module. The marked points should meet.

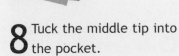

8 Tuck the middle tip into the pocket.

9 This shows two joined modules. Continue adding modules from the right.

Stumpy star

This model is so called because instead of points the arms of the star are blunted. Both sides of the star are equally decorative. To make the star you will need to make five star modules.

1 With the coloured side face up, fold the paper in half diagonally.

2 Fold front flap diagonally to meet the bottom edge. Repeat at rear.

3 Fold the front flap forward.

4 Take the bottom corner to meet the top edge as marked above.

5 Crease flap to the centre line, and then open it up.

6 Take the top corner to meet the bottom edge as marked above.

7 Crease the flap to the centre line and open up.

8 Make a reverse fold at the right.

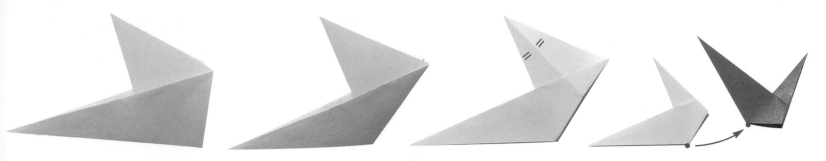

9 Tuck the right-hand tips between the layers.

10 Here is the completed module.

11 Prepare the modules by folding the flaps to the centre, front and back.

12 To join the modules, tuck the flaps of the left-hand module inside the right-hand module. The marked points should meet.

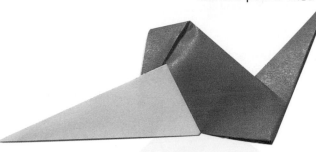

13 Now tuck the middle tip between the layers to lock.

14 This shows two joined modules. Add further modules from the left.

15 The model has to be pulled into three dimensions to complete the joining of the final module. This picture shows the locks on the inside.

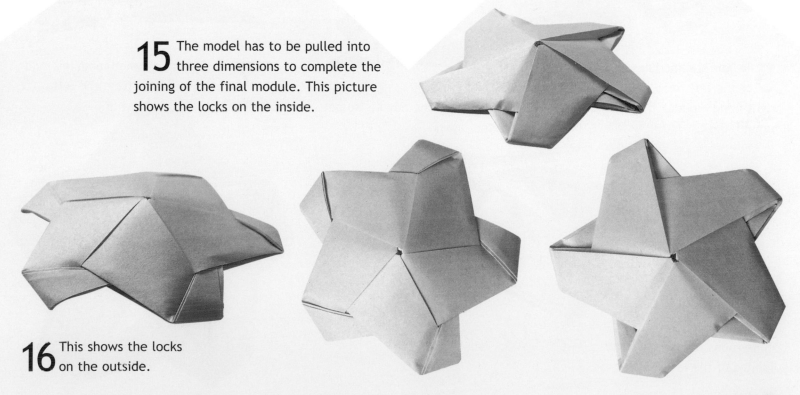

16 This shows the locks on the outside.

Decorated stumpy star ....

This also uses the stumpy-star modules as a base, but adds some folds to create a more decorative finish. You will need five modules. Follow steps 1 to 8 for the stumpy-star before continuing as instructed below.

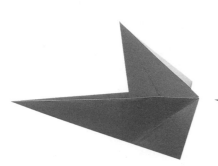

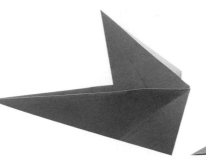

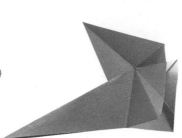

1 Fold and return both the front and rear flaps.

2 Fold and return the right-hand edges, both front and rear.

3 Fold up the bottom corner, then fold down the top flap. Repeat at rear.

4 Your completed module should look like this.

5 To join the modules, tuck the flaps of the left-hand module inside the right-hand module. The marked points should meet.

6 Now tuck the middle tip between the layers.

7 Here are two joined modules. Add further modules from the left.

8 The model has to be pulled into three dimensions to complete the joining of the last module.

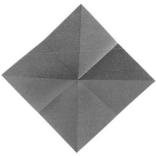

Borealis .... modular designs ◆

This is a complex modular design, and using bright colours makes it a very beautiful model. You first need to create 30 modules.

1 Form a preliminary base (see page 16), with the coloured side outwards.

2 Fold the edges of the front flaps to the centre and return. Repeat at rear.

3 Sink the top point. The crease joins the end of the crease made in step 2.

4 Swivel the right-hand flap to the left.

5 This picture shows the completed module.

6 To join, slide the right-hand module inside the left one.

7 Fold the tip at right angles to lock it.

8 This photograph shows two joined modules.

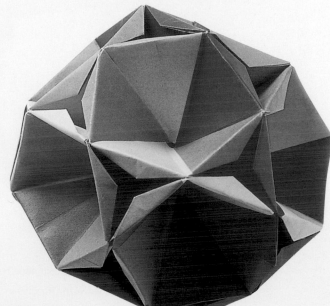

Thirty modules combined create pentagons with triangles on each side.

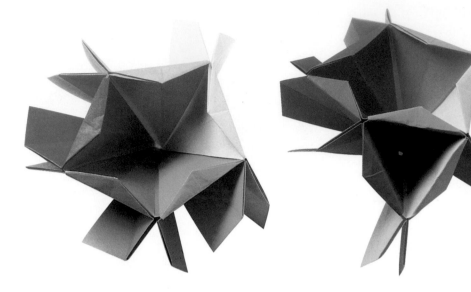

9 Join the modules, starting with a ring of five to form a sunken pentagon. One module is added to each of the two arms at the corners to give small triangles. Eventually every side of each of the triangles forms part of another pentagon.

10 This photograph shows six units joined — a pentagon with a triangle on one corner.

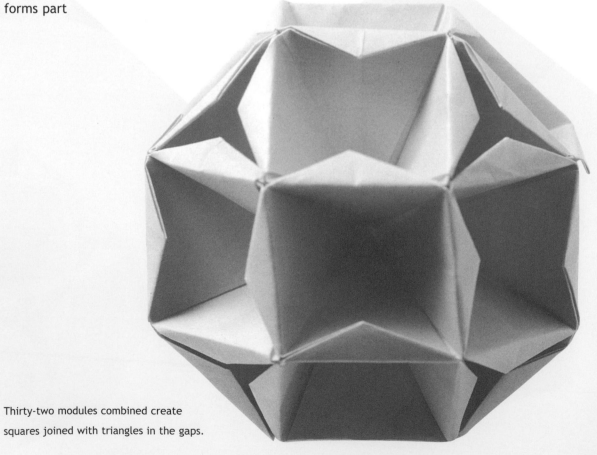

Thirty-two modules combined create squares joined with triangles in the gaps.

Other shapes can be made using the same modules.

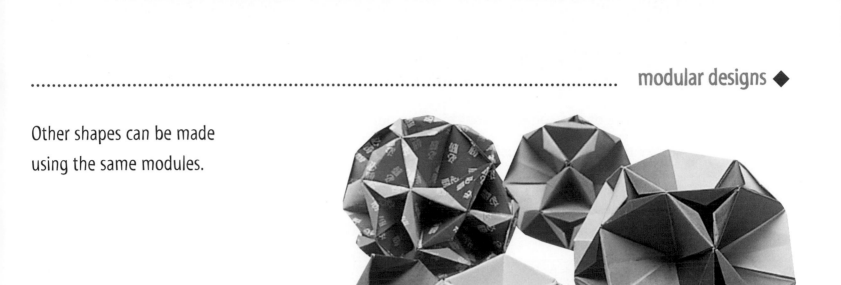

Twenty-four modules combined create a hexagon with triangles on each side.

Four-point star

Two squares are required for this four-point star, folding is different for each. What looks really nice is to use different coloured paper for each square.

Square 1

1 Fold to centre.

2 Fold lower edge to top edge.

3 Fold corners.

4 Fold to centreline.

5 Fold to centreline.

6 Unit complete.

Square 2

1 Fold to centre.

2 Fold top edge to lower edge.

3 Fold corners.

4 Fold to centreline.

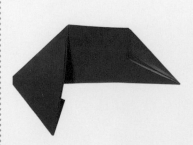

5 Fold to centreline.

6 Unit complete, turn over.

Assembly

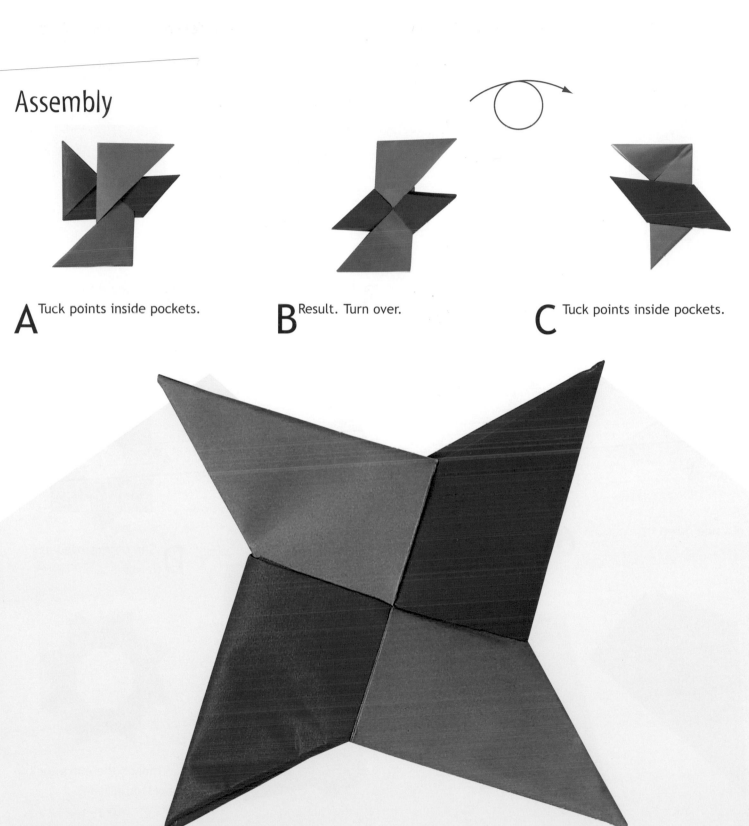

A Tuck points inside pockets.

B Result. Turn over.

C Tuck points inside pockets.

Drinking cup ring

This very simple but effective model creates the perfect accompaniment to any drink.

the fun part is that each segment of the ring is a miniature drinking cup!

1 Fold diagonal.

2 Pinch at top end only.

3 Fold and return. Marked points meet.

4 Reverse fold.

Assembly

5 Fold side down.

6 Tuck tip between layers.

A Tuck tip inside.

D Can be regarded as finished . . .

B Fold flap inside.

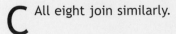

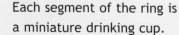

. . .though the extra tuck-in makes variation E.

7 Pleat.

C All eight join similarly.

Each segment of the ring is a miniature drinking cup.

Flight of fancy .... modular designs ◆

This model will make 16, 17, or 18 units. It is best made with an even number to preserve symmetry.

Assembly

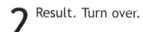

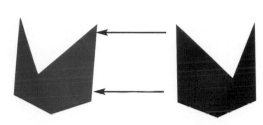

1 Crease diagonal. Fold sides to it.

2 Result. Turn over.

A Insert flaps at rear of one unit into pockets at front of another.

3 Marked points meet; fold only on side opposite marked point.

4 Reverse fold.

B The back of the darker unit lines up with the pocket lining. There is no gap. Here tip of the beak touches top edge of flap. Fold at right angles. Marked points meet. Tuck tip inside.

C Two units joined. Tip of beak touches top edge of flap. Assemble all units similarly.

5 Make 16, the geometrically perfect number. The ring may also be formed with a couple of additional units, then closed and flattened.

front (flight)

back (fancy)

Green cross

This model is based on the British pharmacy logo and is made from four units.

Assembly

1 Fold left edge to centre front, right edge to centre behind.

2 Fold to centreline and return.

A Slide white corner into pocket.

B Fold inside corner using bisector from step 3.

3 Fold and return angle bisector, then inside reverse on crease made in step 2.

4 Fold edge behind, reverse fold at corner.

C Two units joined. All four join similarly.

5 Unit complete. Make four.

Square coaster .... **modular designs** ◆

Another useful model to make and use — a coaster for your morning coffee or afternoon tea.

Assembly

1 Fold diagonal.

2 Fold corner to point and return.

A Tuck point into pocket.

B Fold small triangle inside, and large over it.

3 Inside reverse.

4 Fold top layer down.

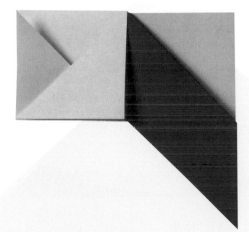

C Completed join. Add remaining units similarly.

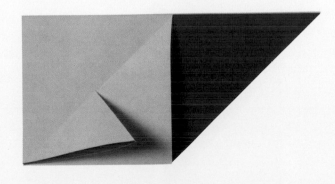

5 Fold along folded edge and return. Make four units.

Back.

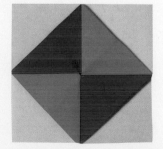

Front.

difficulty :

origin :
Ibolya Tuzy

Flexagon

Flexagons are special structures that change shape when manipulated. Use same-size square for all pieces. It is best to use thicker paper to avoid paper tearing.

Part 1

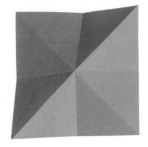 

1 Fold waterbomb base.

2 Fold corners to top point, pinch and return.

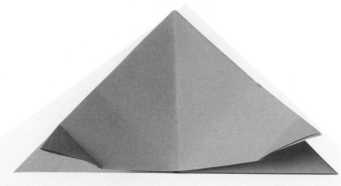

3 Fold corners to pinch mark.

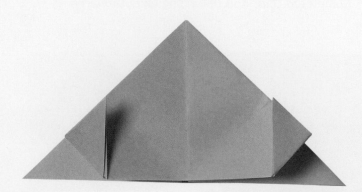

4 Result. Make four.

Part 2

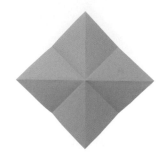 

1 Crease diagonals, then horizontal and vertical.

2 Fold corner to middle, unfold top corner.

3 Fold point to centre.

4 Collapse like the preliminary base.

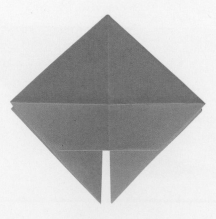

5 Result. Make four.

Assembly

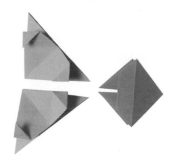

A Insert flaps of first unit into pockets in second unit.
Ensure it is the correct way round so that small triangular flaps go under front pocket.
Large flaps in rear pocket.

B Now fold flap into pocket, behind triangular flaps.

C Result. Units are locked. Add remaining units in the same way.

D Model complete.

START THE ACTION SEQUENCE BY folding corners behind to get a flat square....

fold to get a preliminary base...

rotate out the points....

to get a salt cellar, continue rotating...

continue rotating...

to form a star shape, continue rotating.....

to get a table, continue to return to flat square...

MANIPULATE YOUR FLEXAGON THROUGH ALL ITS SHAPES A COUPLE OF TIMES UNTIL IT BECOMES SUPPLE. YOU CAN THEN TRY GOING BACKWARDS THROUGH THE SEQUENCE.

60° star unit

Follow the same steps for making units for all 60 degree star models. The difference lies in the assembly of each star.

1 Crease centreline.

2 Fold and return, marked points meet.

3 Fold and return, marked points meet.

4 Fold on centreline.

5 Fold and return on existing creases.

6 Inside reverse fold.

7 Result. Turn over.

8 Fold using existing crease.

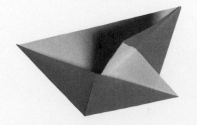

9 Fold to outer edge and return.

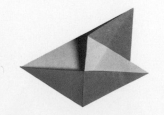

10 Unit complete — make six.

60º star 1 .... modular designs ◆

Follow steps for the star unit on page 150. There are three variations for you to choose from when assembling your star.

Assembly

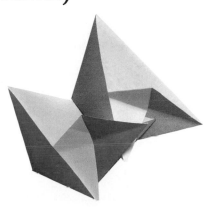

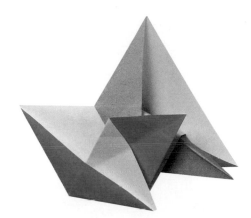

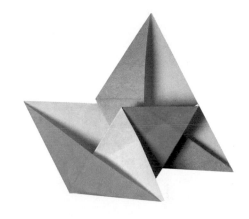

A Rear flap of left unit goes behind front flap of right unit. Marked points meet.

B Fold flap on existing crease.

C Two units joined. All six join similarly.

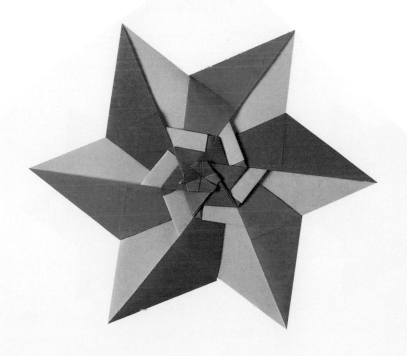

Back of star.

Variation 1

fold points over edge behind.

Back.

Variation 2

Make the creases one by one, then fold all tips simultaneously.

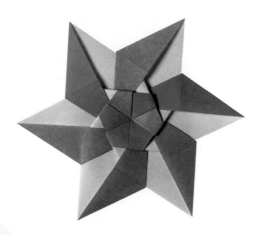

Front.

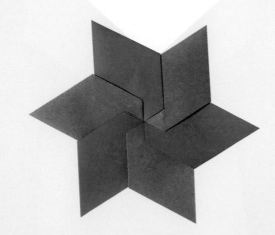

Back.

Variation 3

Start with variation 2. Fold points over edge behind.

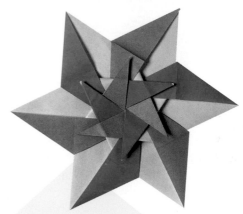

Front.

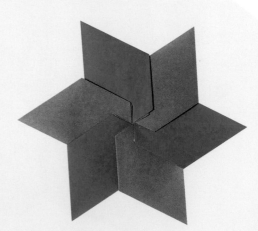

Back.

60º star 2 .... modular designs ◆

Create this beautiful star choosing two colours of your choice. (Don't forget to create the individual units you need to follow steps on page 150).

Assembly

A Flap on left unit goes behind flap on right unit. Marked points meet.

B Fold flap behind inner layers using existing creases.

C Two units joined — all six to join similarly.

D Result. Fold tips behind.

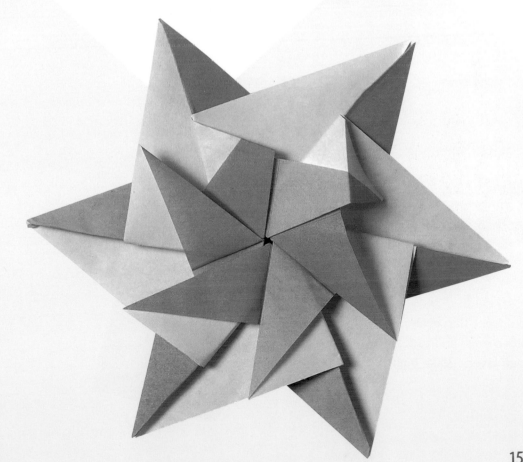

Ring of fire

Ignite your imagination with this model of a ring of fire.

1 Fold diagonal.

2 Pinch only.

3 Fold corner to pinchmark, crease then return.

4 Inside reverse fold.

5 Fold sides down.

6 Fold back edge to top edge. Repeat at rear.

7 Fold front flap over folded edge and tuck between layers. Make eight.

Assembly

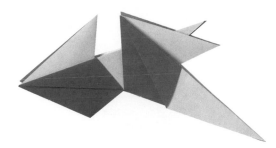 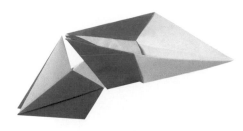 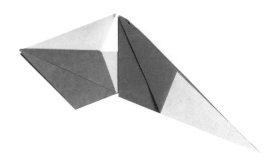

A Tuck flap of one unit into pocket of another — marked points meet.

B Fold central flap between layers.

C Fold rear flap over central flap and tuck between layers.

D Two units joined and the rest join in the same way.

difficulty :

origin :
david petty

Wheel of fire

Wheel of fire is made out of 16 units. Choosing two similar tones of colour for the paper works very well.

1 Fold diagonal.

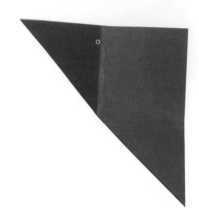

2 Mountain fold point to corner.

3 Fold edge to edge then unfold steps 2 & 3.

4 Inside reverse, then open out.

5 Fold sides to centreline, then turn over.

6 Reform reverse fold.

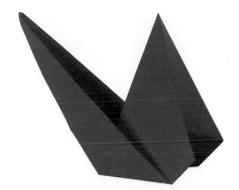

7 Make 16.

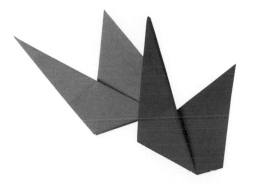

8 Tuck layers of right unit in pockets of left unit. Marked points meet.

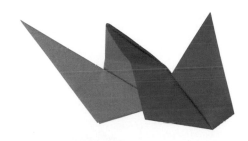

9 Valley fold tip and tuck between layers of right unit. Marked points meet.

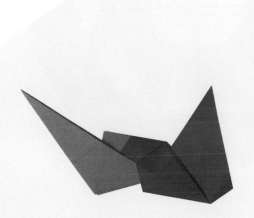

10 Join the remaining units in the same way.

Front.

Back.

Modular construction

(David Petty)

The modular pieces "ring of fire" and "wheel of fire" can be combined provided they are both folded from the same size paper.

Simply locate "ring of fire" inside "wheel of fire". Glue is not required.

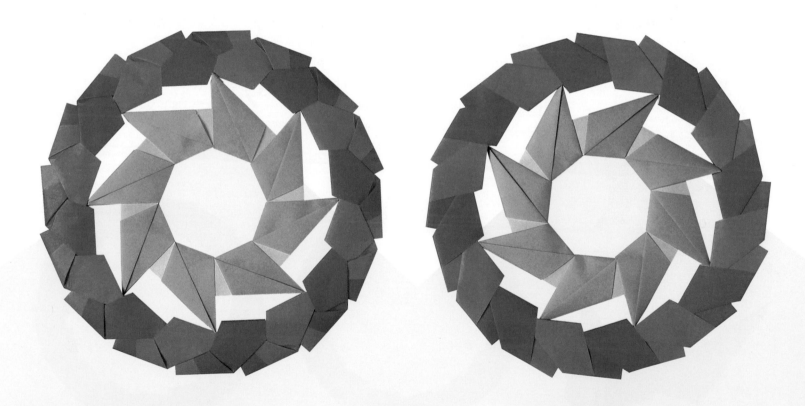

Inner Ring of Fire
Outer Wheel of Fire

Octahedral cross

This really is a very effective model, but as an advanced project the assembly is best done with the aid of paper clips!

1 Crease quarter lines.

2 Crease diagonal only in central sections. Fold sides to centreline. Mountain fold along existing crease.

3 Fold inwards to centre.

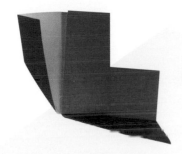

4 Make folds at right angles.

5 Make 12. The best effect is with four units of each of three different colours.

Assembly

Tuck flap of unit into pocket in second unit.

Two units joined, others join similarly.

Assembly is best done with the aid of paper clips!

difficulty :

origin :
david petty

XYZ diamonds

This model has a really structured design. Assembling the first four units is easy — the last two are difficult. A tip: altering the starting paper proportions gives different sized "planes".

1 Crease centreline.

2 Fold sides close to centre; leave a small gap approximately 1mm between edges at centre.

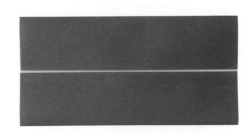

3 Result. Turn over.

4 Crease at centre.

5 Fold to location point. Squash at each end.

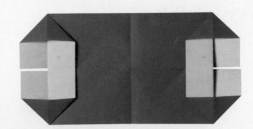

6 Repeat steps 4 & 5 on other end.

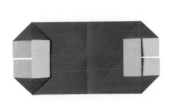

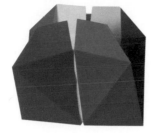

7 Fold in half.

8 Inside reverses.

9 Fold flaps at right angles.

10 Unit complete. Make six (best with two papers of each, with three different colours).

Assembly

Tuck flaps into pockets of neighbouring unit.

Continue adding units in the same way.

5 animals and plants

Here is variety of models from the natural world, including birds, insects and flowers. Children will particularly enjoy creating a miniature menagerie.

Baby rabbit

A cute model that will probably work best with larger paper, as it involves hidden folds that can be tricky to manipulate at a very small scale. It begins with a square, white side face up.

1 Crease both diagonals and then a vertical centre line. Fold both sides to the centre.

2 Now fold the top edge to the centre.

3 Carefully pull out the hidden corners on both sides. Using mountain folds, fold the two top and two bottom corners to the rear.

4 Fold the model in half, using a mountain fold.

5 Rotate the model by 90°. Now reverse-fold the bottom left-hand corner.

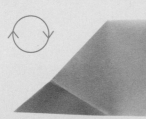

6 Fold the head at an angle to make the rabbit stand upright.

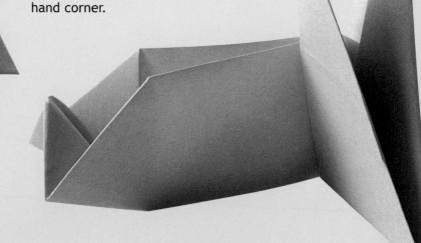

Fat rabbit

.... **animals and plants** ◆

A fun model that requires inflating to complete. It begins with a waterbomb base, made with the coloured side of the paper face up.

1 Form the waterbomb base (see page 15 for full instructions).

2 Fold up the bottom corners of the bottom layer to meet the top corner.

3 Now fold the upper top corners into the middle.

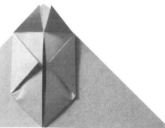

4 Fold down the upper edges of the top layer to meet the folded edges.

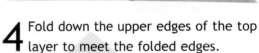

5 Tuck the flaps inside the pockets formed by previous folds.

6 Tuck the flaps in carefully, avoiding creating wrinkles.

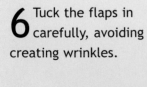

7 Once you have neatly tucked away the flaps, turn the model over.

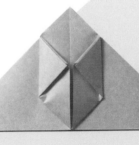

8 Fold the two bottom corners up to the top corner.

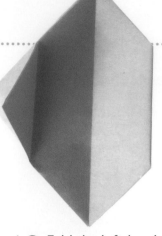

9 Swing the flap over to the opposite side.

10 Fold the left-hand corner of the top layer into the middle.

11 Swing the flap that you have created over to the right.

12 Repeat this step on the other flap.

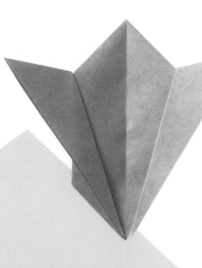

13 Fold out the tips of the model.

14 Take the top layers into the centre.

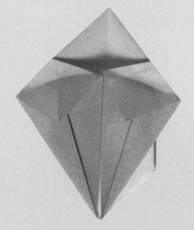

15 Fold up the tips to form ears. Note that the fold only goes part of the way across each ear.

16 Now gently inflate the model from the front to finish your fat rabbit!

Small bird

This amusing three-dimensional model is simple to fold. The inside reverse fold is quite small, so care needs to be taken not to crumple the paper.

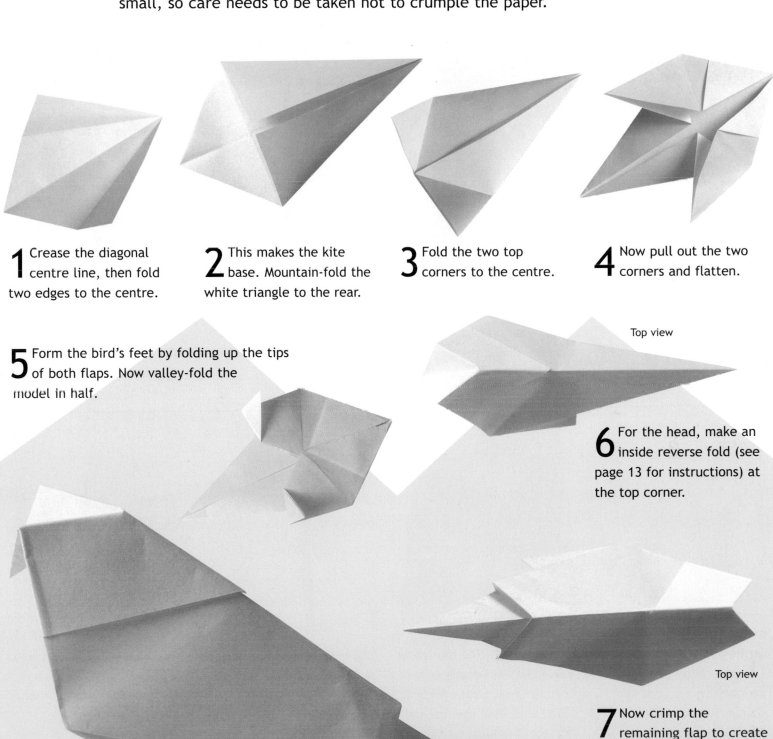

1 Crease the diagonal centre line, then fold two edges to the centre.

2 This makes the kite base. Mountain-fold the white triangle to the rear.

3 Fold the two top corners to the centre.

4 Now pull out the two corners and flatten.

5 Form the bird's feet by folding up the tips of both flaps. Now valley-fold the model in half.

Top view

6 For the head, make an inside reverse fold (see page 13 for instructions) at the top corner.

Top view

7 Now crimp the remaining flap to create the tail. (See page 14 for full crimp instructions.)

Caterpillar

An entertaining model made in three parts — it can be as long as you like. The modules for the body should be made first. Each part requires the same-sized square paper.

body

1 With the white side face up, fold the paper diagonally in half.

2 Fold the left-hand tip of the front layer to meet the right-hand edge.

3 Valley-fold the model in half from top to bottom. This creates your first body segment. Make several of these.

4 To join the body segments, insert the top right-hand corner of one segment over the inside flap of the second segment. Continue until you have as many segments as you wish.

neck

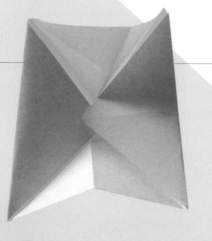

1 Begin with a square with both centre lines creased from corner to corner. Valley-fold the left- and right-hand corners to the centre. Mountain-fold the bottom corner to the rear, also to the centre.

2 Mountain-fold the model in half vertically and return. Make valley folds as indicated. Pull the top and bottom together using the creases you have made.

3 Flatten out the model carefully. The top flap should form an inside reverse, while the bottom tucks inside.

4 To connect the neck to the body, slide it over the top right-hand corner of the first segment.

head

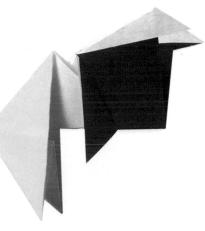

1 Begin with a square with both centre lines creased from corner to corner. Fold each corner to the centre and return.

2 Make mountain folds in both the top and bottom flap, as indicated. Valley-fold the model in half vertically. This creates outside reverse folds at the top and bottom.

3 Now make mountain folds on the right-hand flap, as indicated. Then mountain-fold the model horizontally, working from front to back.

4 This creates the head. Slide it onto the neck to finish your caterpillar.

Grasshopper

Also known as the cicada. This very simple, three-dimensional model makes excellent use of both sides of the paper. It can be very effective when made with glittering foil.

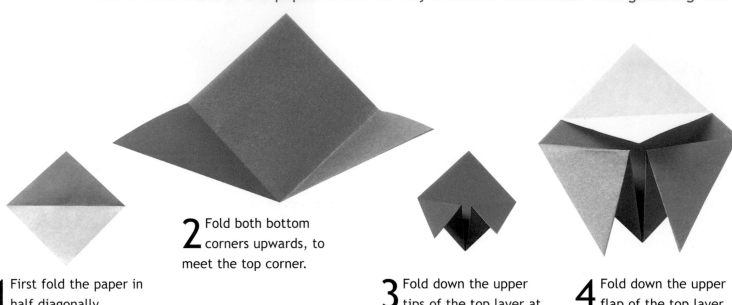

1 First fold the paper in half diagonally.

2 Fold both bottom corners upwards, to meet the top corner.

3 Fold down the upper tips of the top layer at a slight angle.

4 Fold down the upper flap of the top layer.

5 Fold down the upper flap of the bottom layer to the front as well.

6 Fold both sides to the rear at a slight angle. This will make the model stand up.

Pajarita

.... **animals and plants** ◆

This is a traditional European model. Pajarita means 'little bird' in Spanish. The model is known as the 'rooster' in the USA. The flapping action is attributed to Kuni Kasahara.

1 Crease and return the horizontal and vertical centre lines.

2 Then crease and return the diagonal centre lines.

3 Fold the four corners into the centre to form a blintz.

4 Now mountain-fold the four corners to the rear to make a further blintz.

5 Next open out the folded paper fully.

6 To fold the model, first fold along the diagonal of the centre square. The rest of the folds should follow automatically.

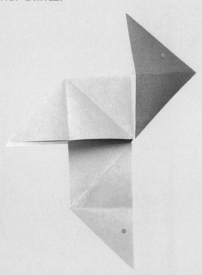

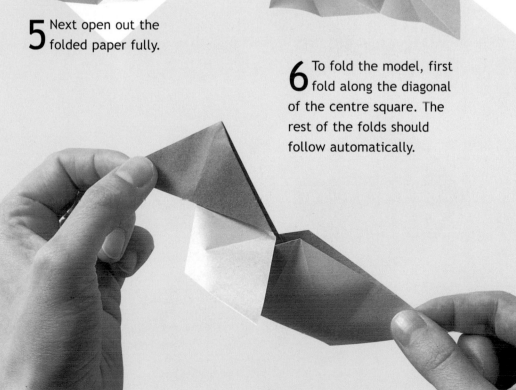

7 This forms your pajarita shape. Either hold it at the points marked or pull and return to flap the wings.

Butterfly

This is a very pretty model, which is particularly effective when made with foil or coloured origami paper.

1 Fold and return both diagonal creases.

2 Fold each of the four corners into the centre.

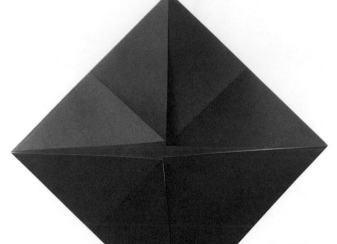

3 This creates a blintz base. Turn this over.

4 Fold and return each of the corners to the centre.

5 Turn the model over again and open out the four corners.

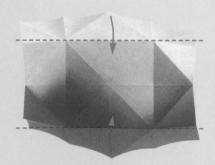

6 Fold the top and bottom edges into the centre.

7 Collapse the model, following the folds as indicated.

8 Mountain-fold the model in half horizontally.

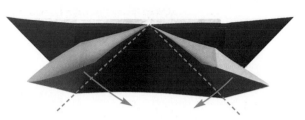

9 Fold down the upper points.

10 Fold in the sides of the flaps.

11 Valley-fold the model in half vertically.

12 Fold both wings to the right at a slight angle.

13 Fold one wing back to the left to complete your butterfly.

Mandarin duck

This attractive three-dimensional model may require some practice as it involves several reverse folds. You may find this easier to do with a large sheet of paper.

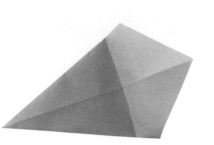

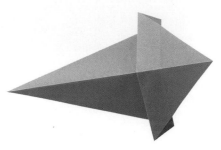

1 First crease a diagonal centre line. Then fold two edges to this centre line to form a kite base.

2 Turn the paper over. Fold in the tip. The corners should not meet.

3 Now fold the white triangle outwards, to the right.

4 Next mountain-fold the model horizontally in half.

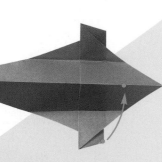

5 Fold up the bottom flap so that the bottom right-hand corner meets the top edge as marked. Repeat at the rear.

6 Make an outside reverse fold with the left-hand tip. The marked points should meet.

7 Next make a further outside reverse fold with this top tip.

8 Form the head and tail by making reverse folds.

Cat face

A series of folds makes up this amusing model. Try experimenting with different folds to see if you can create other animal faces.

1 Crease and return both diagonals. Then fold and return two edges to one of the diagonal creases.

2 Fold and return the top corner. The crease should join the ends of the existing creases.

3 Fold the bottom corner so that it meets the point where the diagonal centre line and the new crease join. Then return.

4 Fold the bottom corner to meet the point where the new crease joins the diagonal centre line.

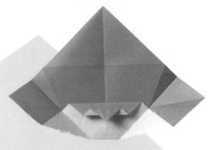

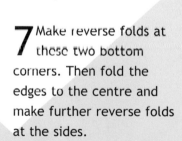

5 Pleat the bottom triangle. Fold the bottom part to the rear, then turn the paper over.

6 Fold and return the bottom corners. Each fold should pass through he intersection of the existing creases.

7 Make reverse folds at these two bottom corners. Then fold the edges to the centre and make further reverse folds at the sides.

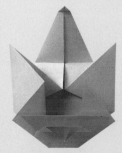

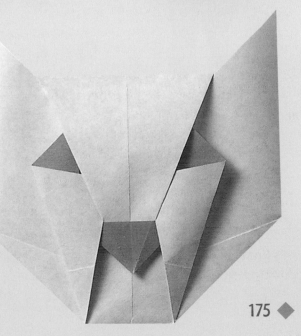

8 Blunt the sharp point at the top, then fold this tip down and tuck it in behind the bottom pleat.

9 Valley-fold the front flaps and tuck them under the central flap.

175 ◆

Plump crane

This three-dimensional model is a quite straightforward version of the traditional crane.

Care must be taken when forming the tail and beak as they are prone to crumpling.

1 First form a preliminary base, as demonstrated on page 16.

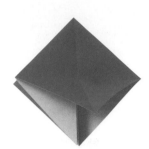

2 Fold up the bottom flap of the front layer to the top corner. Repeat on the process on the rear flap.

3 Fold the left- and right-hand corners of the front layer to the centre. Repeat at the rear.

4 Now fold the sides, both the front and the back, into the centre.

5 Reverse-fold the front and rear. Make an additional reverse fold near the tip of one of the long points to make the beak.

6 Spread out the wings and flatten the top of the model.

Flapping bird 1 .... animals and plants ◆

A fun model that can be made to move – make the folds carefully!

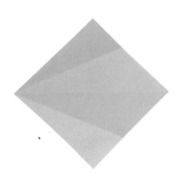

1 Fold sides to centre.

2 Fold white triangle in.

3 Turn over.

4 Fold one third, allow back flap to flip.

5 Fold in half.

6 Fold lower sides to rear, squash small triangles.

7 Reverse folds.

8 Hold firmly at A and pull tail B down and return to flap wings.

Winking crab

A variation of an original model, using paper of different colours on each side to create the winking effect. For a uniform crab, use paper of the same colour on both sides.

1 With the white side face up, crease a diagonal centre line. Mark the centre of this line and then fold the top and bottom corners to the centre.

2 Fold the two corners out at a slight angle.

3 Now valley-fold the model in half.

4 Fold up the left- and right-hand corners.

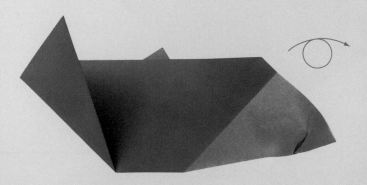

5 Mark a crimp in the right-hand crab claw.

6 Unfold the claw and pull out the paper from the rear.

7 Turn the model upside down to complete the crimp and return flap.

8 Fold the flap back up to the top.

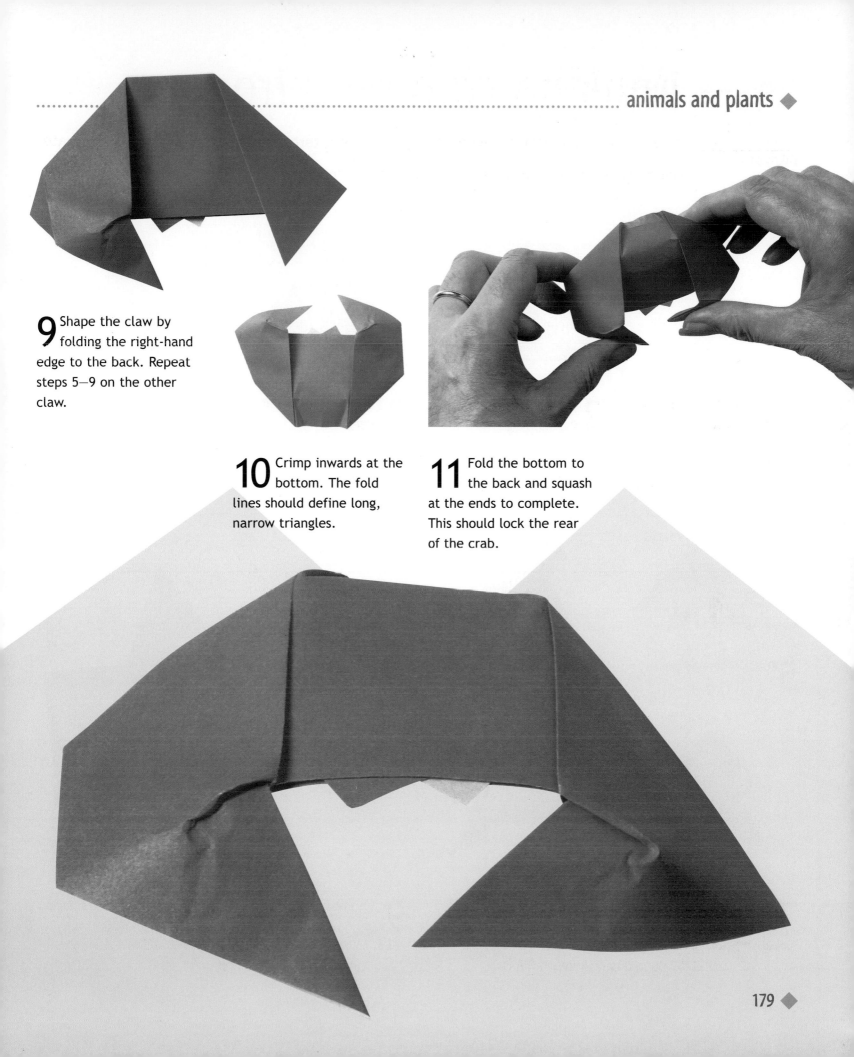

9 Shape the claw by folding the right-hand edge to the back. Repeat steps 5—9 on the other claw.

10 Crimp inwards at the bottom. The fold lines should define long, narrow triangles.

11 Fold the bottom to the back and squash at the ends to complete. This should lock the rear of the crab.

American jumping frog

This is a traditional model which begins with a waterbomb base. You will really enjoy watching this frog unfold; be careful it doesn't hop away!

1 Form waterbomb base.

2 Fold sides to centre.

3 Fold sides to folded edge.

4 Result. Turn over.

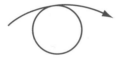

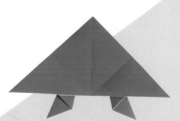

5 Fold corners to point.

6 Fold corners to side points.

7 Fold corners to make feet pleat to form spring.

8 Result. Turn over.

9 Complete. To operate — run finger down the frog's back.

Carrier pigeon

A pigeon shaped container!

1 2 x 1 form water bomb in lower part. Pleat top part.

2 Squash fold.

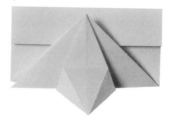

3 Petal fold.

4 Valley fold.

5 Valley fold.

6 Repeat steps 2—5 on right-hand side.

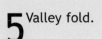

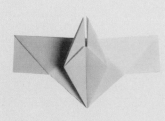

7 Mountain fold.

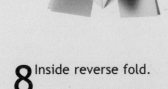

8 Inside reverse fold.

9 Punch holes to tie with thread. Complete.

Bird

This quite intricate three-dimensional model makes good use of both sides of the paper as it comes alive and takes flight.

1 White side up, make a fish base.

2 Mountain fold in half.

3 Open and squash.

4 Open and squash.

5 Valley fold flap.

6 Valley fold, marked points meet.

7 Valley flaps front and back.

8 Reverse fold.

9 Reverse fold.

10 Open out to step 8.

11 Valley fold, marked points meet.

12 Fold down so that the edge passes through the bottom corner.

13 Unfold steps 11 & 12.

14 Reverse fold using existing crease.

15 Colour change.

16 Reinstate reverse folds from steps 8 & 9.

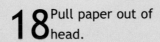

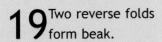

17 Outside reverse fold and crimp wings.

18 Pull paper out of head.

19 Two reverse folds form beak.

Goldfish

This is a really delightful yet simple model to fold.

1 Fold a diagonal.

2 Fold side points to centre point.

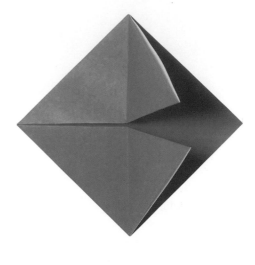

3 Fold points to top point.

4 Fold out both points.

5 Valley fold top layer only.

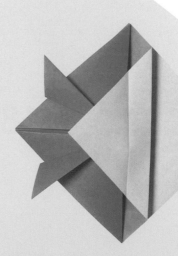

6 Valley fold top layer only.

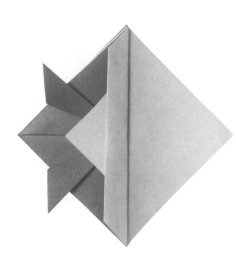

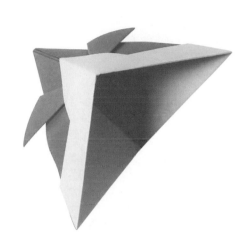

7 Mountain fold flap to rear.

8 Pull layers apart, then flatten.

9 Cut approximately two thirds way on both bottom edges.

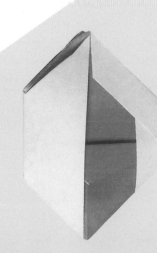

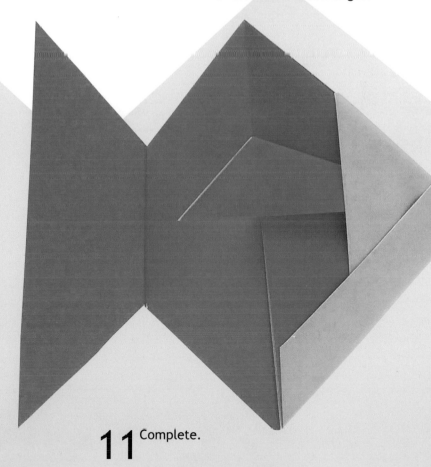

10 Peel back top layer and flatten.

11 Complete.

Flapping bird 2

This is another amusing model of a bird in flight. Care needs to be taken on the reverse fold at step 7, as this can be quite small.

1 Make an inside reverse fold at the right-hand corner. Make a further inside reverse fold at the tip of the flap that you have just created.

2 Make another inside reverse fold at the left-hand corner.

3 Fold the bottom flaps, front and rear layers, to the top to form the wings.

4 Valley-fold the back edge of the front wing down to the horizontal. Repeat at the rear.

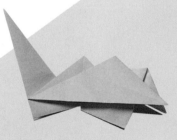

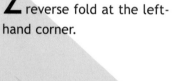

5 Now gently spread out the wings.

6 Press at the back of the wing to break the ridge. Repeat at the rear.

7 To flap the wings, hold the model at the points shown and pull on the tail. Return to your starting position. Work the mechanism gently until it has been bedded in, after which it is possible to make rapid wing beats.

Egg-laying hen .... animals and plants ◆

This is well worth folding and great fun too, as the farmhouse hen

looks as if it's laying an egg.

1 Form preliminary base.

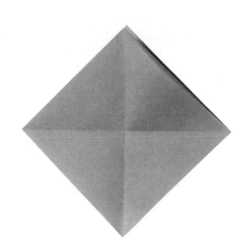

2 Fold point down, repeat at back.

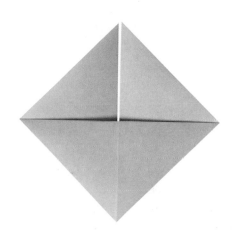

3 Book fold.

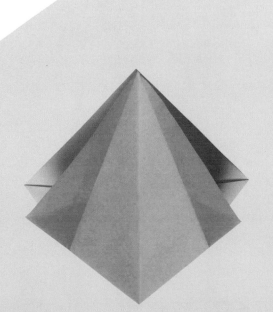

4 Fold sides to centre, front and back.

5 Book fold.

6 Inside reverse.

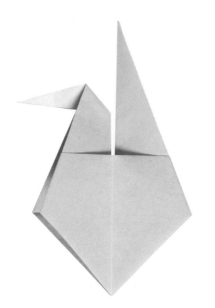

7 Outside reverse.

8 Inside reverse.

9 Inside reverse.

10 Inside reverse.

11 Fold flaps up.

12 Tuck flaps in.

13 Cut off point.

14 Fold corners between layers, front and back.

15 Egg complete.

16 Slide egg between flaps.

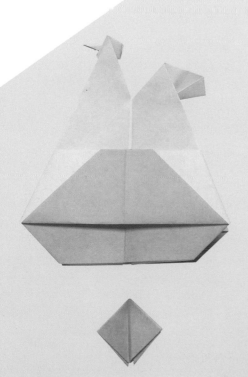

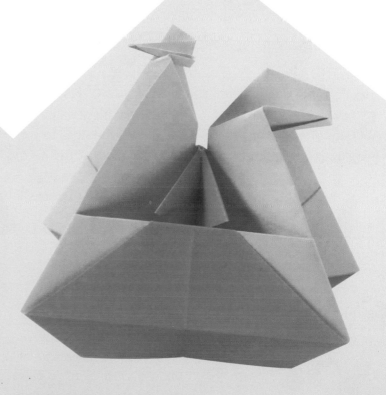

17 Egg emerges.

18 Work head and tail up and down.

Autumn leaf

A group of these leaves can make a very pretty display, and the autumn leaf is quite easy to fold. It begins with a square with both diagonal creases folded and returned.

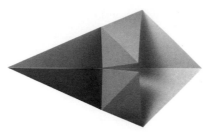

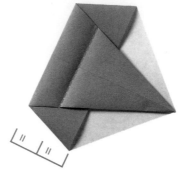

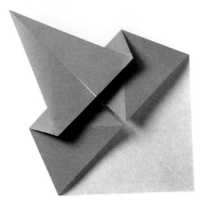

1 Fold two of the edges to one of the centre diagonal creases.

2 Valley-fold the model in half horizontally.

3 Fold back the front tip at the halfway point on the lower coloured layer.

4 Pull out both lower flaps from under the central layers.

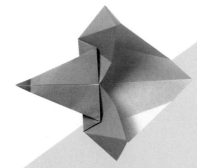

5 Reverse-fold both side flaps. Fold the top tip inwards to blunt the tip.

6 Narrow the stalk by folding the sides to the centre. Squash at the bottom corners (see page 11 for squash instructions).

7 Fold the stalk at an angle and blunt the corners of the main part of the leaf. Turn over. To make the leaf stand up, fold and return both top corners.

Frog .... animals and plants ◆

This fun three-dimensional model needs care and attention to avoid crumpling. The model will require inflating at the end. It begins with a frog base (see page 21).

1 Bring the left-hand front flap to the right. Repeat the process at the rear. This is a book fold.

2 Fold the lower edges to the centre line. Repeat at the rear.

3 Book-fold the model once more, as in step 1.

4 Fold the lower edges to the centre line. Repeat at the rear.

5 Now make a further book fold.

6 Make inside reverse folds on the upper layers as far up as the paper will allow. The outer edge should lie on the existing edge.

7 Make inside reverse folds on the flaps that you have just created, left and right.

8 This picture shows how the model should look at this stage.

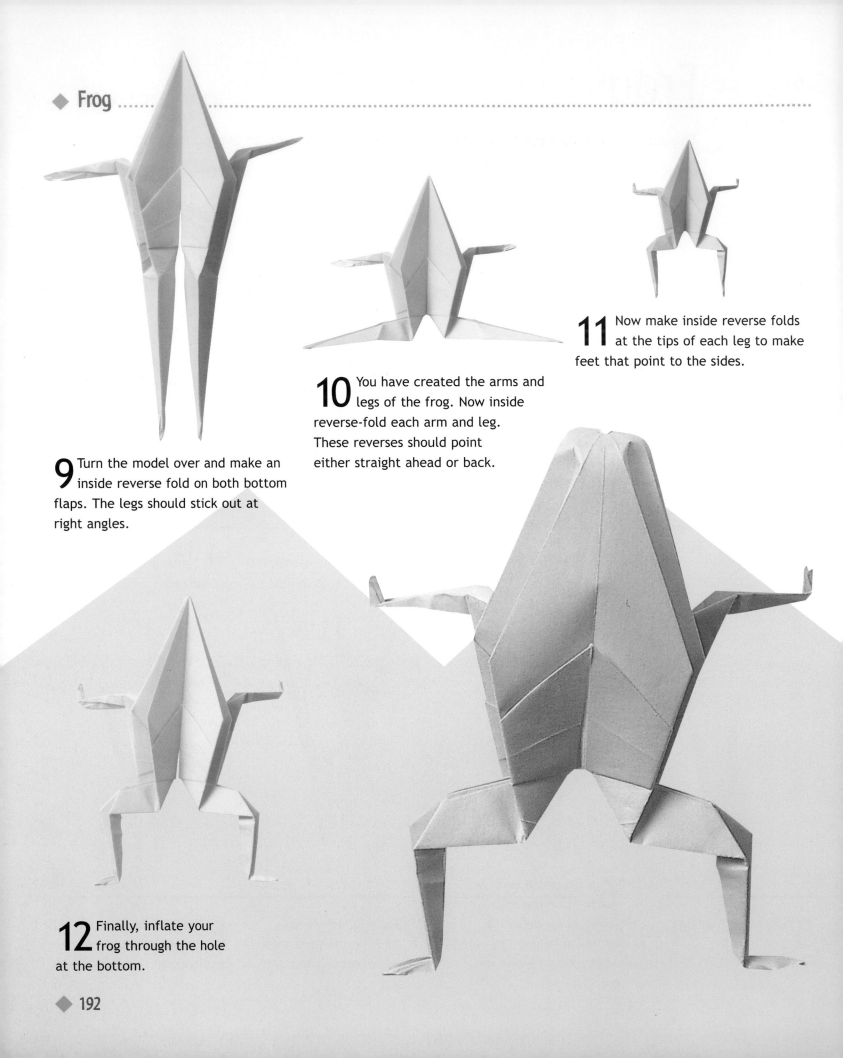

11 Now make inside reverse folds at the tips of each leg to make feet that point to the sides.

10 You have created the arms and legs of the frog. Now inside reverse-fold each arm and leg. These reverses should point either straight ahead or back.

9 Turn the model over and make an inside reverse fold on both bottom flaps. The legs should stick out at right angles.

12 Finally, inflate your frog through the hole at the bottom.

Snail

.... **animals and plants** ◆

This three-dimensional model is one of the most difficult to complete successfully. It also requires care to avoid crumpling. Practise several times on scrap paper before using proper origami paper.

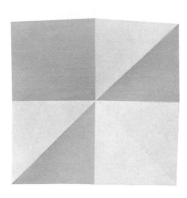

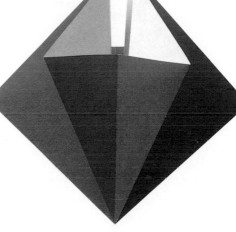

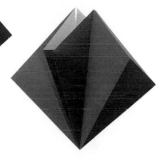

1 With the white side face up, first form a preliminary base (page 16).

2 Squash the right-hand flap at the front and also at the back.

3 Bring the right-hand flap over to the left for a book fold. Repeat at rear.

4 Squash the remaining right-hand flap. Repeat at the process at the rear.

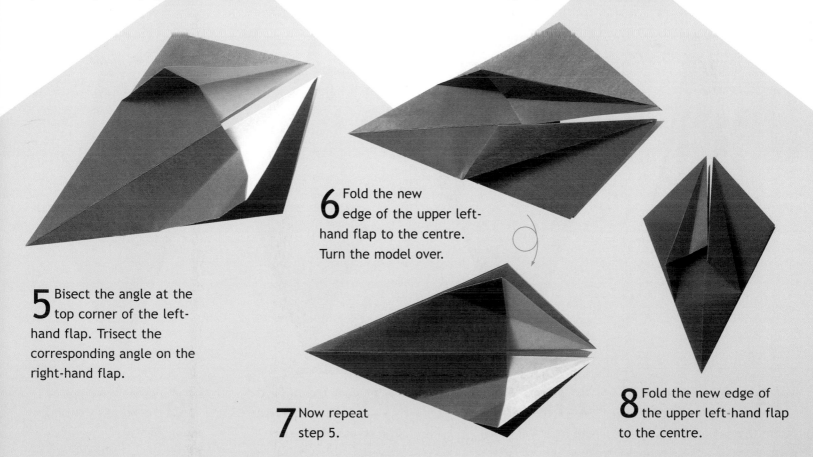

6 Fold the new edge of the upper left-hand flap to the centre. Turn the model over.

5 Bisect the angle at the top corner of the left-hand flap. Trisect the corresponding angle on the right-hand flap.

7 Now repeat step 5.

8 Fold the new edge of the upper left-hand flap to the centre.

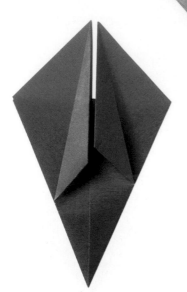

10 Bisect the angle at the top corner of the left-hand flap. Trisect the corresponding angle on the right-hand flap. Now repeat at the rear.

9 Book-fold the left-hand flap to the right and repeat at the rear.

11 Next fold the flaps at both the front and the back.

12 Book-fold the right-hand flap to the left and repeat at the rear.

13 Reverse-fold the left- and right-hand tips to form the snail's horns.

14 Tuck the tip of the front flap between the layers of paper.

15 Tuck the tip of the rear flap between the layers of paper.

16 Adjust the angle of the horns by raising them slightly.

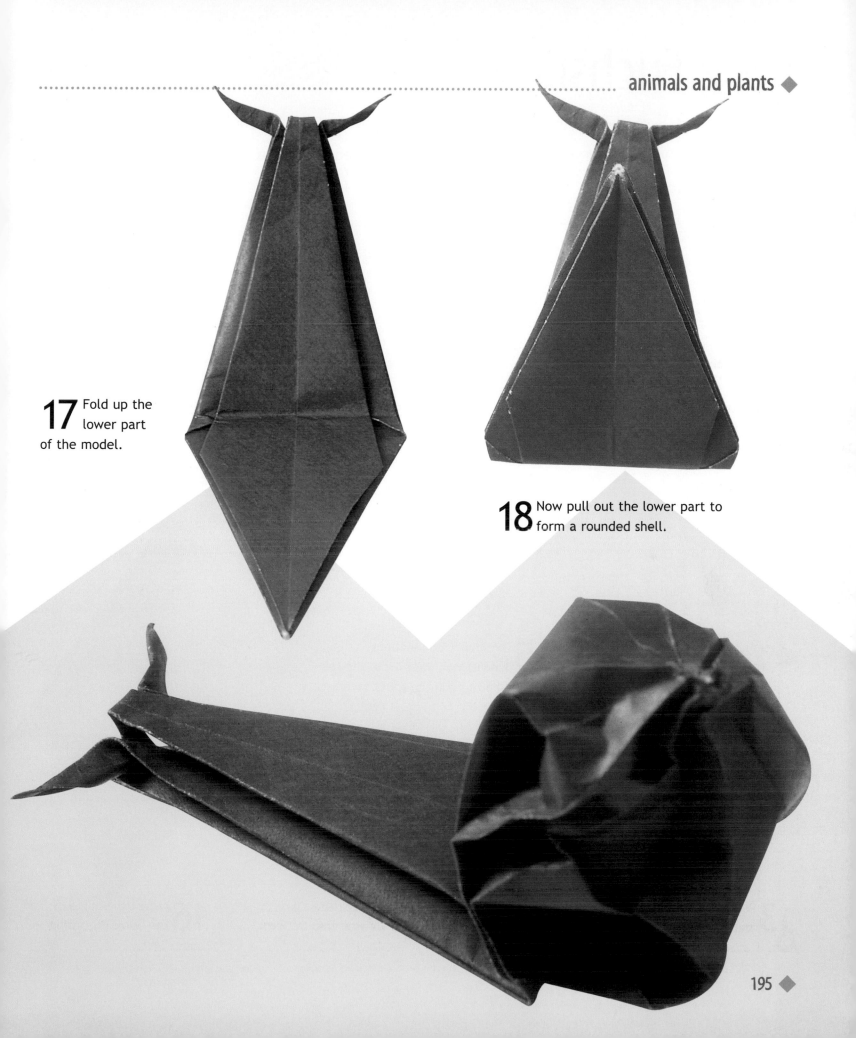

17 Fold up the lower part of the model.

18 Now pull out the lower part to form a rounded shell.

Fuchsia

As with the fall leaf, these models form a lovely display if you group several of them together. Because you will need to make a number of complex folds, try working with larger paper first.

1 With the paper's white side face up, form a preliminary base.

2 Squash-fold each of the flaps in turn.

3 Fold in the edges by about one third, then return. Repeat on all flaps. Open out the paper.

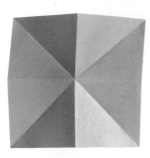

4 Pleat one section of the sheet along the existing crease lines.

5 The model is now three-dimensional. Valley-fold the top layer and squash the lower layer.

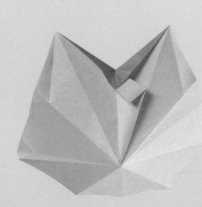

6 Repeat step 5 on all four sides.

7 This shows an inside view of the fuchsia.

difficulty :

👍 👍

origin :
David Petty

Sunflower

The beauty of this model is that with your own choice of coloured paper you can create your very own bunch of flowers.

1 Form preliminary base.

2 Squash all four flaps.

3 Swing one flap across, repeat.

4 Fold point up, repeat at rear.

5 Swing flap across, repeat at rear.

   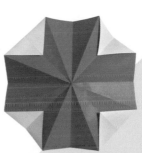

6 Fold tip up, repeat at rear.

7 Result; open out, leaving white triangles folded.

8 Result, turn over.

9 Marked points meet; make eight creases.

10 Make eight more creases.

11 Collapse using existing creases.

12 Fold triangles into pockets.

13 Centre complete, two pockets in each segment.

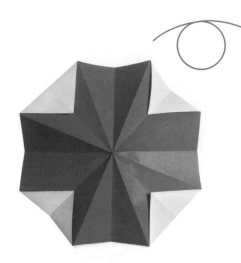

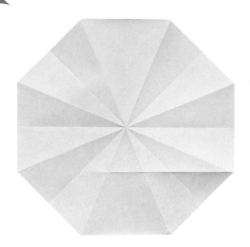

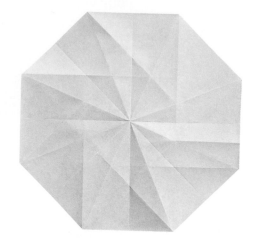

8 Result. Turn over.

9 Marked points meet. Make eight creases.

10 Make eight more creases.

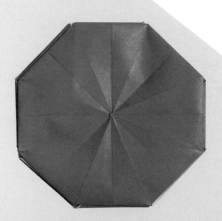

11 Collapse using existing creases.

12 Fold triangles into pockets.

13 Centre complete, two pockets in each segment.

Petal

1 Fold sides to diagonal.

2 Fold sides to diagonal.

3 Rabbit-ear at point where inner layer meets edge.

4 Squash.

5 Colour change.

6 Tuck flaps under.

7 Result. Turn over.

8 Complete. Make 16.

Assembly Tuck petals into pockets in centre. Two variations are possible.

I made my sunflower from 6 x 6cm (15 x 15in) (yellow) petals.and 10 x 10cm (4 x 4in) (black or brown) centre.
Do you want leaves? Then fold as petal in green. Don't like sunflowers?

Persimmon

Why not recreate this unusual fruit, but remember it's only edible when fully ripe!

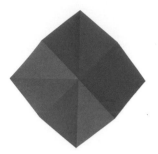

1 Form preliminary base.

2 Fold and return, repeat at back.

3 Squash. Repeat on all four flaps.

4 Bookfold front and back.

5 Fold down point.

6 Fold corners behind — repeat steps 5 & 6 on remaining points.

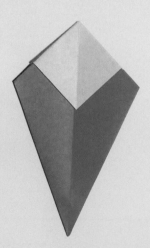

7 Inflate.

difficulty :

origin :
David Petty

Tree

These models form a lovely display if you group several of them together.

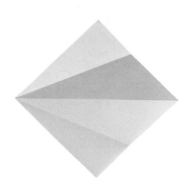

1 Green down, brown up, crease diagonal, then fold sides to the crease.

2 Fold sides to crease.

3 Rabbit-ear from point at which inner layer meets edge.

4 Squash.

5 Colour change.

6 Petal fold.

7 Fold tip up, then turn over.

◆6 transport

A selection of cars, boats, trains and a plane. Many of these models are quick and easy to make, although the 3D models require more patience and practice.

Jet plane

Although this is an easy model to fold, you need to make the creases and angles accurate, otherwise your jet will not fly.

1 Crease a central diagonal line. Now fold two of the edges to this centre line.

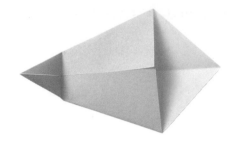

2 This gives you a kite base. Valley-fold the tip about one-quarter of the way along the diagonal.

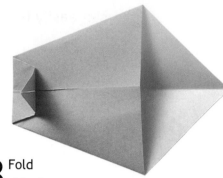

3 Fold this tip back, leaving a pleat.

4 Valley-fold the model in half.

upside down

5 Fold down the wings at right angles from the plane body and turn over. Your plane should now be ready to fly.

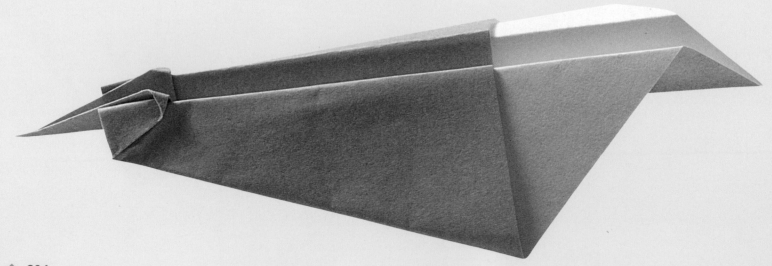

Train set

The next projects allow you to create an entire train set, comprising an engine, a carriage, a flat truck and a goods wagon. You can make as many of the last three models as you wish. This folding routine is the basis for several transport models and can easily be adapted to make vehicles of your own.

engine

1 Crease the centre line vertically. Fold the paper horizontally, but do not crease it. Now make a small pinch at the centre.

2 Fold the bottom edge to meet this pinch at the centre.

3 Fold down the corners of this bottom flap. Note that the folds do not go all the way into the corners.

5 Fold down the right-hand corner. The fold starts a short way up the front and ends parallel to the bottom edge.

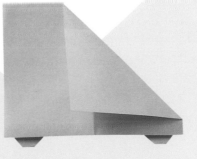

4 Blunt these bottom corners by folding the very tips up. Turn the model over.

6 Mountain-fold the top part to the rear to complete your engine.

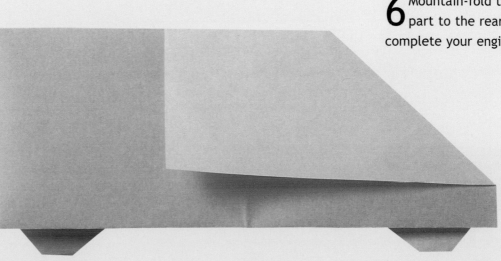

carriage

1 Crease the centre line vertically. Fold the paper horizontally, but do not crease. Make a small pinch at the centre.

2 Fold the bottom edge to meet this pinch at the centre.

3 Fold down the corners of this bottom flap. Note that the folds do not go all the way into the corners.

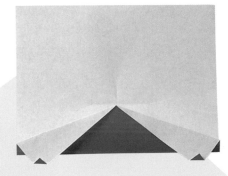

4 Blunt these bottom corners by folding the very tips up. Turn the model over.

5 Fold down the top edge. This fold should leave a coloured strip below when complete. Fold the top corners to the rear to finish.

flat truck

1 Crease the centre line vertically. Fold the paper horizontally, but do not crease it. Now make a small pinch at the centre.

2 Fold the bottom edge to meet this pinch at the centre.

3 Fold down the corners of this bottom flap. Note that the folds do not go all the way into the corners.

4 Blunt these bottom corners by folding the very tips up. Fold down the top edge.

5 Fold the two bottom corners to the centre crease.

6 Fold the bottom tip up to the top edge, then turn over to finish.

goods wagon

1 Crease the centre line vertically. Fold the paper horizontally, but do not crease it. Now make a small pinch at the centre.

2 Fold the bottom edge to meet this pinch at the centre.

3 Fold down the corners of this bottom flap. Note that the folds do not go all the way into the corners.

4 Blunt these bottom corners by folding the very tips up. Fold down the top edge to touch the centre point.

5 Next fold up the bottom edge of the top flap.

6 Inside reverse both top corners (see page 13 for full instructions).

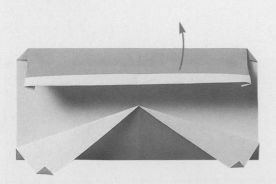

7 Fold the ends of the top band inside. Fold up the flap and turn the model over to finish.

Van

This model uses the same basic technique as the train set. With some experimentation, you can create a fleet of cars of your own design.

1 Crease the centre line vertically. Fold the paper horizontally, but do not crease. Make a small pinch at the centre.

2 Fold the bottom edge to meet this pinch at the centre.

3 Fold down the corners of this bottom flap. Note that the folds do not go all the way into the corners.

4 Blunt these bottom corners by folding the very tips up. Turn the model over.

5 Fold the top edge down so that it lines up with the flaps at the rear. Mountain-fold one of the top corners to the rear to complete your van.

Yacht

A number of small folds are needed for this model, so it is probably better to use a large-sized paper. This model begins with the paper coloured side face up.

origin :
David Petty

1 First crease both diagonal centre lines and then return.

2 Fold the left-hand and top edges to meet the diagonal crease and then return.

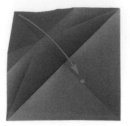

3 Fold the top left-hand corner from where the two creases meet. The tip of the corner should lie on the diagonal crease.

4 Fold back the tip, making the fold along the line that has been formed between the ends of the existing creases.

5 Mountain-fold the edges of the triangle to the rear.

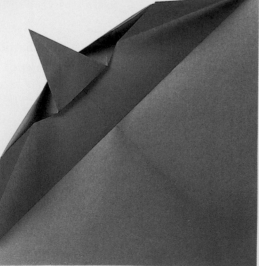

6 Fold down both corners on either side of the triangle, working along the existing creases.

7 Fold up the right-hand and bottom edges to make the yacht's hull. This can be as deep as you wish. Now reverse-fold the model.

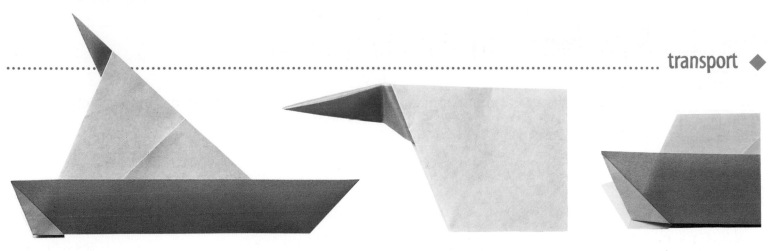

8 This gives you your basic yacht shape.

9 Now crimp the flag inside, so that it points to the side.

10 Fold the back flap of the top layer inside the model.

11 Fold the back flap of the bottom layer inside the pocket you have just created. Finally, spread the bottom layers to make your yacht stand upright.

French automobile

This is another variation on the previous models. It captures the distinctive appearance of the classic French 2CV.

1 Crease the centre line vertically. Fold the paper horizontally, but do not crease. Make a small pinch at the centre.

2 Fold the bottom edge so that it meets this pinch at the centre.

3 Fold the corners of this bottom flap down. Note that the folds do not go all the way into the corners.

4 Blunt these bottom corners by folding the very tips up. Fold the top down so that the edge touches the centre.

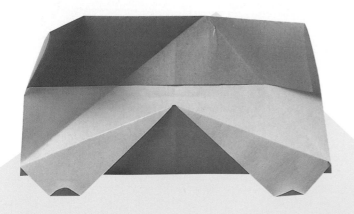

5 Fold down the top left-hand corner. Then fold in the right-hand corner. Finally, fold in the new left-hand edge.

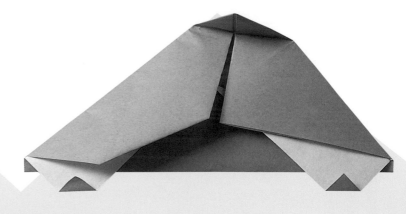

6 Blunt the top corner to complete the shape, then turn over.

Chinese junk

.... **transport** ◆

A traditional fishing boat. As with the sampan, this model involves complex folds. The final pulling step will have to be done gently to avoid tearing the paper.

1 With the white side up, blintz your paper.

2 Fold the top and bottom edges to the centre.

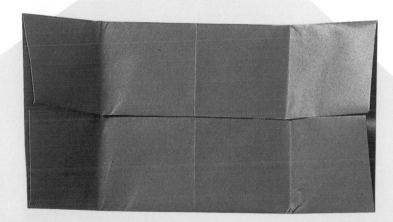

3 Now old the left- and right-hand ends into the centre.

4 Fold the four inner corners to the outer edges and return. Now pull out the inside points.

5 Mountain-fold the sides behind to the centre.

6 Now open up and spread the top layer.

7 Make squash folds at the top and bottom.

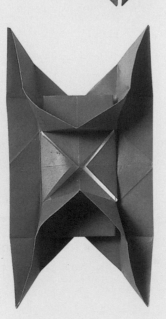

8 Carefully pull out the blintzed corner from the centre at the sides.

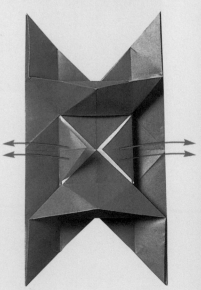

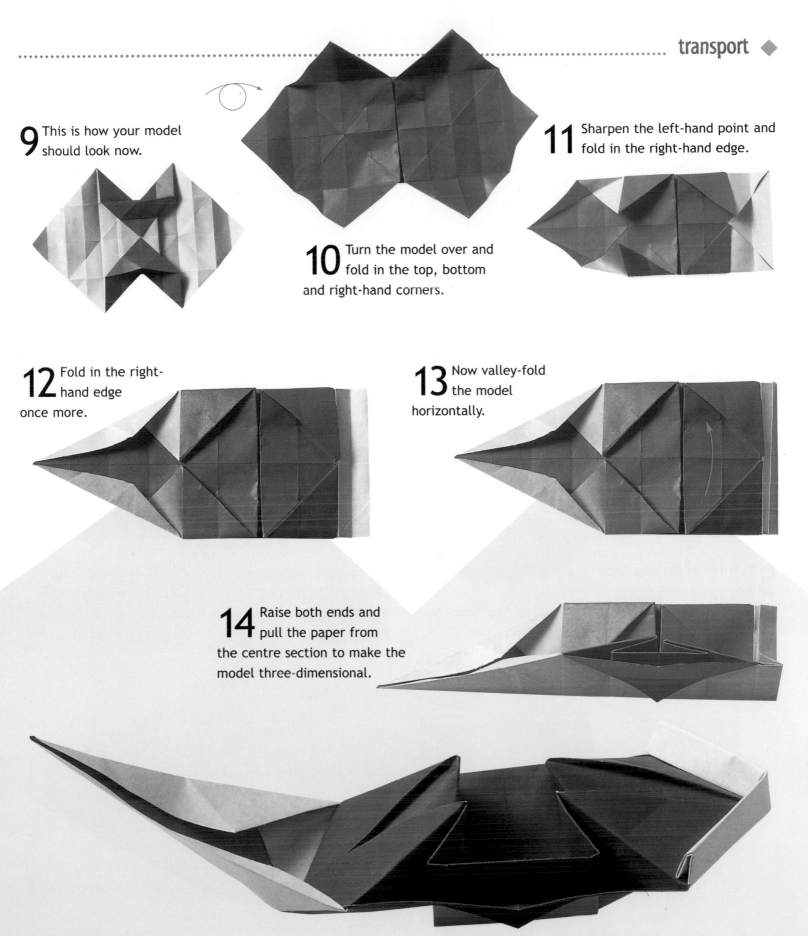

9 This is how your model should look now.

11 Sharpen the left-hand point and fold in the right-hand edge.

10 Turn the model over and fold in the top, bottom and right-hand corners.

12 Fold in the right-hand edge once more.

13 Now valley-fold the model horizontally.

14 Raise both ends and pull the paper from the centre section to make the model three-dimensional.

Sampan

This is a traditional Japanese boat. The model has some complex folds and needs to be pulled into three dimensions. You should use thin, strong paper.

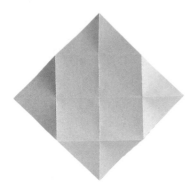

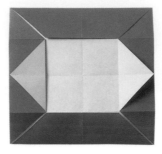

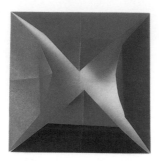

1 With the white side up, blintz your paper.

2 Fold all four corners to the outside edge. Two opposite corners lie inside the other two outside.

3 Mountain-fold the top and bottom edges.

4 This is the shape you should end up with.

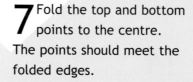

5 Turn the model over and fold the corners to the centre line.

6 Fold all four edges to the centre line.

7 Fold the top and bottom points to the centre. The points should meet the folded edges.

8 Pull from the inside to turn the model inside out. This can be tricky, so pull gently to avoid tearing.

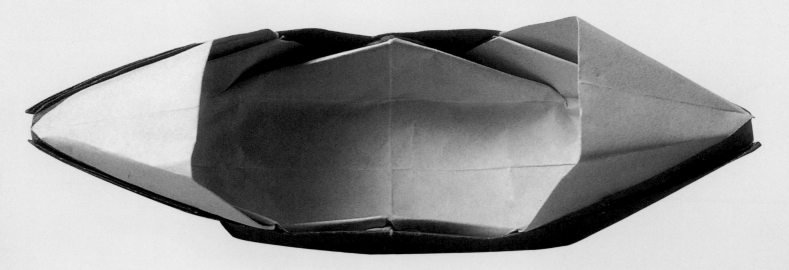

Sailboat 1 and 2 .... **transport** ◆

The white and blue side of the paper together really bring these little boats to life; but remember they don't really float!

1 Fold in half on diagonal.

5 Fold tip down, turn over.

1 Fold corners to centre.

3 Fold bottom corner to centre.

2 Fold points to centre of bottom edge.

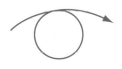

2 Raise sides.

4 Fold tip down, turn over.

3 Fold triangles up.

6 Complete. Rear triangle will form a stand.

4 Fold bottom corner to centre.

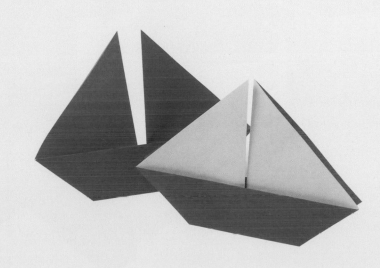

5 Complete.

7 complex models

The following projects include creating a three-dimensional model by using a series of narrow folds. Maintaining the accuracy of the folds requires plenty of practice and patience, so these models deserve their own chapter!

difficulty :

origin :
David Petty

Vase

Although this model is not too difficult itself, maintaining fold accuracy makes it tricky to complete successfully. Use different-sized paper to create larger or smaller models.

1 With the coloured side face up, crease the paper horizontally, but do not fold — pinch at the centre only.

2 Crease the bottom edge to the pinch and return.

3 Mountain-fold a new crease to meet the first crease and return.

4 Now crease and return the horizontal centre lines.

5 Mountain-fold a crease at the top. The strip should be the same size as at the bottom.

6 Now pleat vertically into sixteenths. Take the time to keep all of the strips even.

7 Now fold up the bottom edge. Then reverse-fold the three bottom strips.

8 This shows a side view, with two of the sections folded back down.

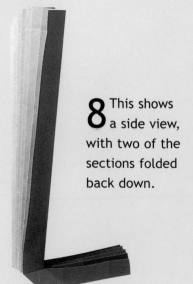

9 Bring both sides together to form a column.

10 Overlap two strips all the way along the edges.

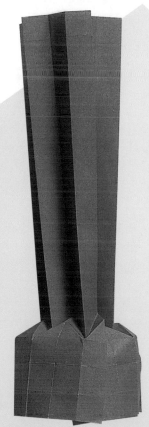

11 Now fold in one section at the top and one at the bottom to complete.

Pine cone

This is one of the most complex models to create as it requires precision and patience to make the many small folds. You will need to begin with the coloured side of the paper face up.

1 Precrease the square into sixteenths and pleat in the centre.

2 Make alternate valley and mountain folds to form a tube.

3 Interlock the flaps. Overlap two of the sixteenths at each end.

4 This shows the tube completely joined.

5 Reverse out all of the side flaps (28 in all). It is best to do one section at a time, unfolding each section to gain access to further sections.

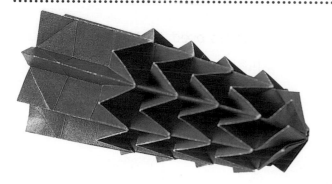

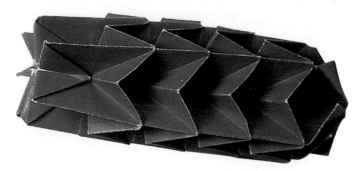

9 Next inside reverse-fold all of the bottom corners.

11 This shows all of the bottom flaps folded. Now shape the sides by stretching them.

10 Fold up all seven triangular bottom flaps.

difficulty :

origin :
David Petty

Cactus in a pot

An even more complex design than the pine cone! It requires a 2 x 1 rectangle, and you will need to start with the coloured side face up. Use a large size of paper.

1 Precrease the rectangle, folding the top half into sixteenths and the bottom half into quarters x eighths. Pleat the top section and make diagonal creases in the two rows above the final row of the top section.

2 Mountain-fold the bottom edge behind. Then valley-fold this folded edge to the central crease. The fold that you have just made should bisect the row. Pleat the top section.

3 Bring the sides together. Form waterbomb bases using the diagonal creases created at the end of step 1.

4 Now join the two edges together carefully.

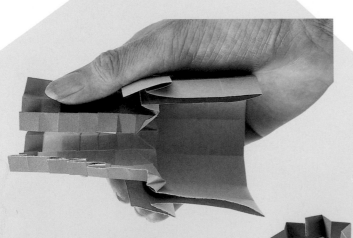

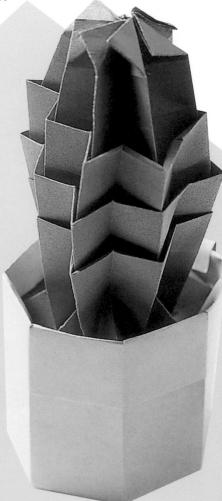

5 Interlock and overlap two of the sixteenths all the way down the join (it is possible!)

7 Turn the top corners over to lock. Then stretch each top flap to shape the cactus.

6 Tuck the top and bottom edges of the pot inside to lock.

3D Christmas tree .... complex models ◆

An advanced project for the more experienced folder as it requires precision and patience to make the many small folds.

1 Precrease into eighteenths.

2 Pleat as indicated.

3 Fold edges down in order. Produce points where marked P follows steps 4-6.

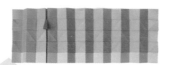

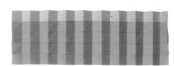

4 Form a pleat, then unfold and reform while pushing top edge down and pulling bottom edge forward. Picture shows this partway.

5 Point complete.

6 Unfold all points to return to step 4. Pleat, then curl ends together.

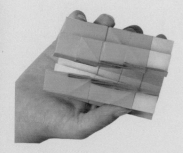

7 Interweave and overlap 2/18ths. Re-form pleats to form eight fluted columns.

8 Refold the points from steps 5–7. Fold top tips inside.

Pineapple

This model is intended for the more practiced folder. You will need to begin with orange and brown paper.

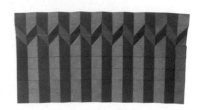

1 Precrease into sixteenths.

2 Fold top 2/16th behind, and make pleats at 3rd, 6th and 9th creases.

3 Pleat, valley-mountain etc.

4 Reverse folds.

5 Side view of result of step 4. Curl ends round.

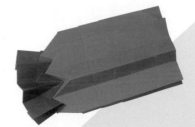

6 Interlock layers, and overlap every second 16th.

7 Inside reverse crease bottom corner.

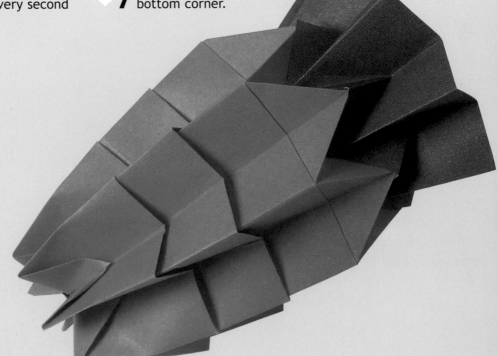

8 Fold up bottom flaps to lock base. Shape by stretching the sides.

WXYZ modular .... complex models ◆

This makes 12 units. The best effect is when each triangle in the final model is of a different colour. For this, use three units in each of four different colours.

1 Pinch in centre and lower edge.

2 Creases here only. Unfold to white side up.

3 Pinch quarter mark at edge.

4 Fold in half.

5 Marked points meet.

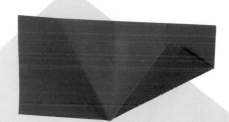

6 Fold to meet edge.

7 Edges meet.

8 Unfold and . . .

9 . . .fold to other corner.

10 Squash.

11 Fold to back.

12 Unfold.

13 Squash.

14 Fold to back.

15 Fold flaps along raw edge (repeat at back).

16 Lift flaps to stand at right angles.

17 Make 12 units.

Assembly

Flaps in one unit go inside pocket in next unit.

Assembly can be tricky (you can get lost) and the best method is to join four units in a ring, then extend each colour into a triangle.

difficulty :

origin :
David Petty

Tensegrity module variation ....

This makes 12 units. The best effect is when each triangle in the final model is of a different colour: for this use three units in each of four different colours.

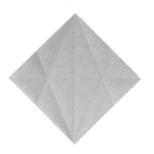

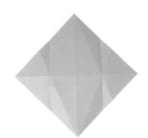

1 Precrease diagonals as valleys from white side, then fold and return edges to one diagonal.

2 Fold and return.

3 Collapse.

4 Fold flaps along line of edge.

5 Fold flaps to centre.

6 Fold edge to outer edge, repeat at rear.

7 Unfold side flaps.

8 Squash fold flaps.

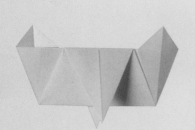

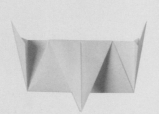

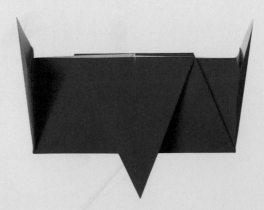

9 Rotate, squash, and fold flaps to be at right angles to the main body.

10 Module complete.

11 Make as many as required.

One flap of right module tucks into pocket of left module.

Two modules joined.
Remainder join similarly.

Variation

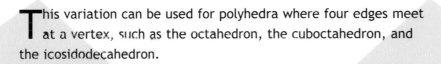

This variation can be used for polyhedra where four edges meet at a vertex, such as the octahedron, the cuboctahedron, and the icosidodecahedron.

For the cuboctahedron (12 modules), each half of each module is common to a triangle and a square, with triangles and squares alternately round a vertex (the centre of the module). Similarly, for the icosidodecahedron (30 modules) the faces are triangles and pentagons alternately at the centre of a module.

The clever module design is by Ian Harrison. Whilst folding his modular pieces, I came across a surprise. Expecting to produce a regular prism, I discovered a twisted piece which I dubbed "maypole", because of the twist and the colours. This piece has also been called "stack-o-stars".

51 modules

Start at one end with a ring of three modules, add further modules, with alternate rings of four and three to form an end cap. The body is formed from rings of four, complete with end cap in mirror image. End caps are half cuboctahedrons.

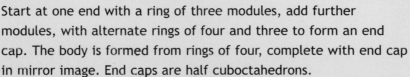

The twist comes naturally and does not have to be encouraged.

120º unit

The model is based on a cuboctahedron, and has four six-point star planes. Use paperclips to stabilise the structure during assembly.

1 Precrease.

2 Fold corners to centre.

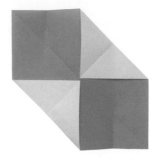

3 Pinch in halfway creases.

4 Mountain fold.

5 Marked points meet. Fold and return.

6 Mirror crease in top part of flap. Repeat steps 5 & 6 on rear flap, then open out.

7 Collapse on existing creases.

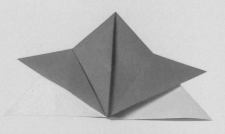

8 Asymmetrical squash.

9 Turn over, and make the same squash on left-hand side.

Assembly

Joining the units together leaves a white triangle on the right within the triangular dimples when using standard origami paper.

Start with a ring of three units, then extend each unit into a six-pointed star plane. A fourth plane (blue in the illustration) is added halfway. Each triangular ring is surrounded by four unit rings.

The model is based on a cuboctahedron, and has four six-point star planes. Paperclips are useful to stabilise the structure during assembly.

10 Rotate squashed flaps to 90°.

11 Unit complete. Make 12.

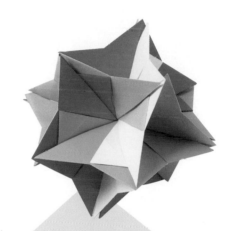

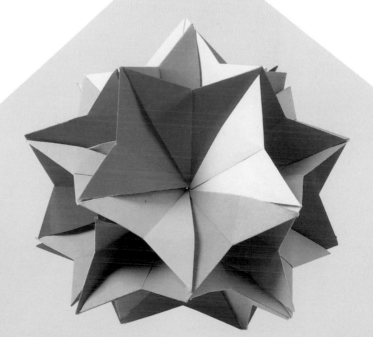

90º unit

The model is very loosely based on a pentagonal anti-prism ring. Paperclips are useful to stabilise the structure during assembly.

1 Mountain fold.

2 Fold corners to centre.

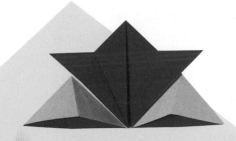

3 Mountain fold.

4 Rabbit-ear fold and return. Repeat on rear flap, then open out.

5 Collapse on existing creases.

6 Squashes.

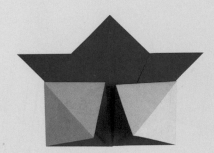

7 Rotate squash flaps to 90°.

8 Unit complete. Make 20.

Assembly

Flaps of right unit tuck into pockets in left unit.

Two units joined. All 20 join similarly.

White shows on right within some rings, when using standard origami paper.

Start with a ring of five units, each a different colour. Extend each side into a ring of three units to make another similar ring with extended sides (using a reversed direction of joining). Join the two structures, one upside down, to the other, to give five eight-point star planes.

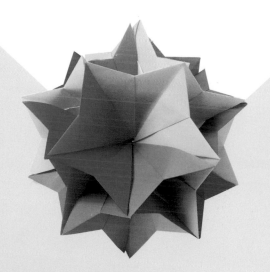 

The model is very loosely based on pentagonal anti-prism ring. The structure is:-
5
33333
44444
44444
33333
5

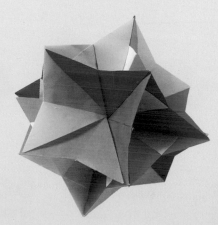

Borealis variation

This really is something to aspire to! Because it's skeletal in its shape and patterned it is perhaps more effective than Borealis (see page 139).

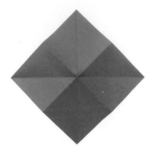

1 Form preliminary base.

2 Fold sides to centre and return.

3 Sink top point.

4 Fold point to centre of top edge. Repeat on all four sides.

5 Swing front flap to other side.

6 Decorated unit one complete. Make 30 (or 24 or 18).

6a For plain unit, tuck triangles under.

6b Plain unit complete make 30 (or 24 or 18).

6c For alternative decorated unit, fold edges of white triangles behind.

6d Decorated unit two complete. Make 30 (or 24 or 18).

6e For alternative decorated unit, fold only one edge of white triangles behind.

6f Decorated unit three complete. Make 30 (or 24 or 18).

Assembly

(same principle for all units)

A Tuck one flap inside the other.

B Fold tip at right angle.

C Two units joined.

Join the units, starting with a ring of five to form a sunken pentagon. One unit is added to each of the two arms at the corners to give small triangles. Eventually each side of the triangles forms part of another pentagon. Pay attention to the white areas. Best results are when all units within each pentagon are similar. Unlike borealis, this modular piece is skeletal and patterned, which makes it more dynamic.

Here's a selection of completed models using the different
units, including colour reversal of units. Constructions are
from 30, 24 or 18 units.

index

credits & acknowledgements

GUEST CREATORS

Acknowledgement is given to the following creators who gave permission for their work to be included in this book.

Tun Ken Lam — British, with a mathematical bent, his modular creations are fine examples of original and economical folding.

Ian Harrison — British, also with highly developed mathematical side, his creations tend to be geometric.

Ibolya Tuzy — Hungarian, she too demonstrates originality and economy in her models.

Edwin Corrie — British, known for animal models.

Nick Robinson —

PAPER

Most models in this book are designed to use standard origami paper which is coloured one side and white on the other. The final model will demonstrate if the white side of the paper is designed to show. Some models will turn out fine using paper the same colour both sides. My advice is to use the cheapest paper you can find (brown paper, copier paper, wrapping paper, newspaper etc.) when folding a model for the first time. If it goes badly wrong, then not much is lost. When you have learnt the model, then use the more expensive paper.

There are extensive ranges of origami paper available. Ranging from Japanese washi (expensive), through patterned and foiled papers (less expensive), to plain colour and duo coloured paper (less expensive still). Packs of paper intended for modular work are available, usually in smaller sizes, with many sheets of the same colour. Beware of patterned papers — it can sometimes be hard to see the creases required to fold the model correctly.

There are several internet sources of paper too — auction sites as well as book sellers.

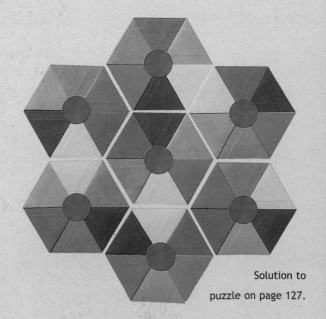

Solution to puzzle on page 127.